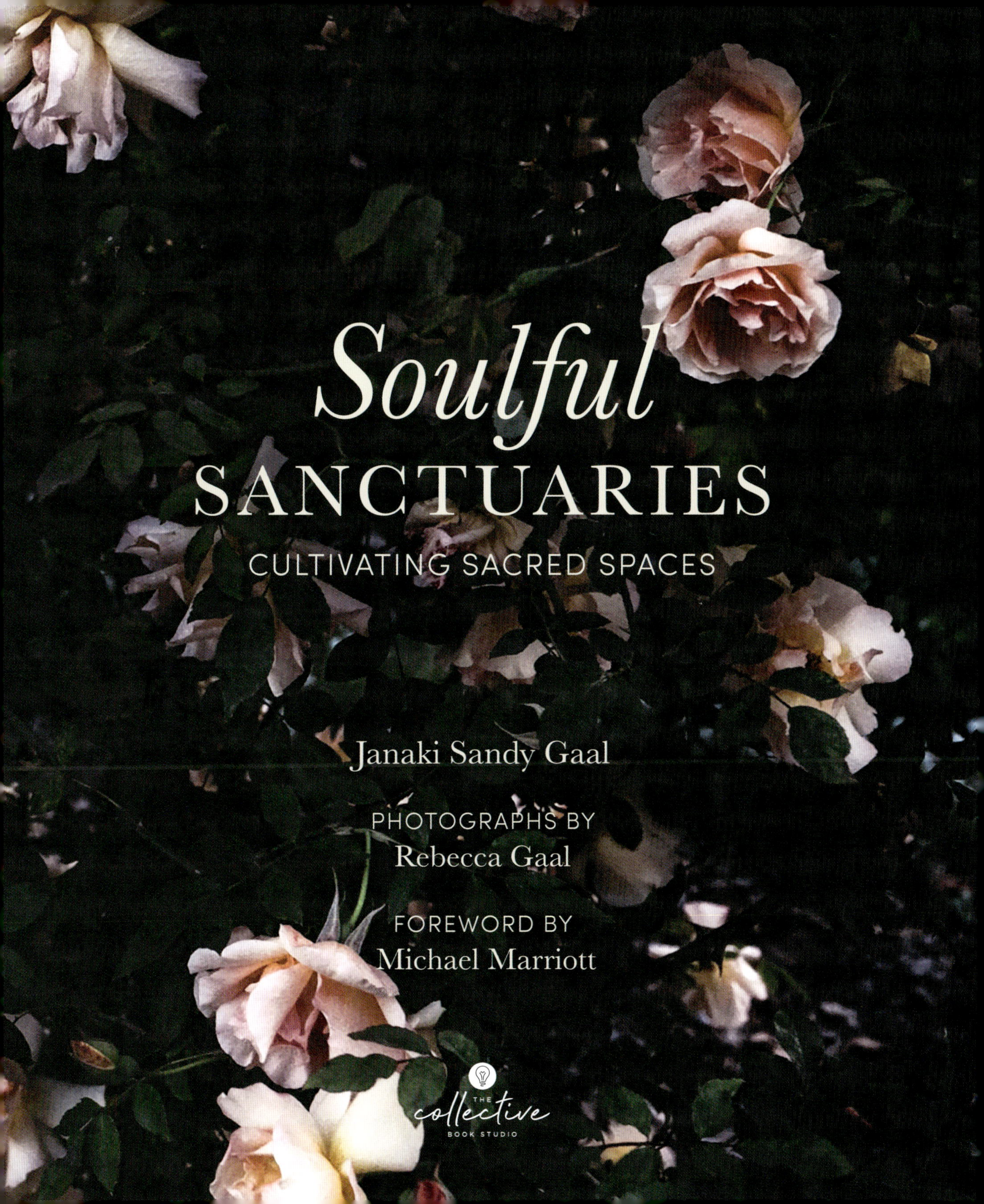

Soulful SANCTUARIES

CULTIVATING SACRED SPACES

Janaki Sandy Gaal

PHOTOGRAPHS BY
Rebecca Gaal

FOREWORD BY
Michael Marriott

THE collective BOOK STUDIO

All photographs by Rebecca Gaal unless otherwise credited.

Library of Congress Cataloging-in-Publication Data available.
ISBN: 978-1-68555-178-0
Ebook ISBN: 978-1-68555-847-5
Library of Congress Control Number: 2026904055

Illustrations by Laura Baxter,
except for garden drawings on page 26, 98, 113 by Nick Williams.
Additional photographs:
Page 221 by Baldo Villegas
Page 205 by Jeri Jennings
Pages 34, 70, 73, 91, 172, 199, 201, 203, and 207 by Syl Arena
Edited by Rebekah Piatte.

10 9 8 7 6 5 4 3 2 1
Manufactured in China

Design by Rachel Lopez Metzger

The Collective Book Studio®
Oakland, California
www.thecollectivebook.studio

"This is a garden of memories.
Walk gently and lift your heart to God."

—ANONYMOUS

To my husband, Peter Gaal:

He never promised me a rose garden, but for 30 years he so generously supported my garden, my dreams, and always encouraged me to follow my heart. It was such a blessing to have him for my partner in life.

To my spiritual teacher, Ram Dass:

He so sensitively guided my life for 50 years. He always encouraged me, not only to follow my heart, but to write from it. He is my sweet inspiration and the Master Gardener of my spiritual heart.

To my daughter, Rebecca Janaki Gaal:

This book would not exist if it weren't for the devotion and capabilities of my daughter, Rebecca Gaal. Becky offered to be my project manager! In addition, her creativity and talent as a photographer has brought a unique beauty to this book. She has been part of this garden since before she was born, and her help to make this book a reality feels like the completion of a beautiful circle.

To each of my incredible gardeners:

Who, over the years, with their gardening skills, hard work, and dedication, have loved the garden into being and translated my garden dreams into reality: Juan Ornelas Flores "Parocco," Camilo Orozco, Francisco Vargas, Juan Vargas #1, and his nephew Juan Vargas. They are part of our family.

To Ganga Ma, Marlene Roeder:

Who helped me love this book into being. Beloved friend, one of my greatest teachers, and my first editor. She left her body one week before we completed the manuscript.

To Neem Karoli Baba "Maharaj-ji":

I have been given so much Grace. This book is an attempt to share that Grace.

CONTENTS

FOREWORD BY *Michael Marriott*

I have been a keen gardener from a very early age, even going on to study agricultural botany while at university. I worked in the South Pacific for five years and then joined David Austin Roses back in 1985, first as nursery manager and then, later, as head rosarian. I advised gardeners around the world on every aspect of rose growing—including designing rose gardens. Though now retired, I continue to advise, lecture, and write about roses. So I can honestly say I have visited many thousands of gardens over the years. Some have stayed with me, while others were soon forgotten. Sandy's is one that I do remember, even though it has been a long time since I was last there.

It is relatively easy to create a garden: It is simply a matter of planting an array of plants, perhaps with an area of grass or paving to sit on. But to create a beautiful garden with soul, as Sandy has, is so much more difficult and achieved only by few. It is quite easy to recognize such a garden. You can often feel it as soon as you walk through the gate, but to say why it is special is much more challenging. It is a sign that the gardener really loves their plants and understands them—that they have worked with Mother Nature rather than trying to impose their will over her. It also shows that they have thought deeply about their garden both as a whole and in detail. It should be the aim of every gardener.

When Sandy first opened her garden to the public, many visitors recognized how special it was and came up to her saying how peaceful it felt—despite sharing it with more than a thousand other people. I had the advantage of being there alone with her, and her love and passion for the garden, the plants, and especially the roses, shone through.

Sandy has indeed created a very special garden and she is a very special person. This book is an extremely valuable guide to gardeners who would like to create their own special garden.

'Gertrude Jekyll®' (English, 1986)

INTRODUCTION: THE *Heart* OF *This Story*

I have a story to tell you. It is the evolution of the soul of a garden—my garden. It is an acre full of charming gardens, primarily made of roses, that flow from one area to the next, leading you along a path through spaces of wonder and delight.

The life and soul of any garden is intimately intertwined with that of the gardener. With work, attention to detail, love, and grace, the garden becomes a reflection of the gardener's inner journey.

When I visit another garden—or even read a garden book, as you are doing now—I look for inspiration, pictures, and ideas. I search for new ways to translate my dreams into reality. I ponder what works and what doesn't work and why. I look for examples to help me imagine the appearance of my own garden over time.

My intention in writing this book is not only to explore the parallels between my spiritual journey and the way it has manifested in my garden, but also to get you excited about gardening and help deepen your appreciation of the spiritual dimensions of life. There is an intimate multifaceted interrelationship between the two, like the gnarled trunk of an Old Garden Rose.

This is not just a spiritual book, and it's not just a gardening book, either. Its uniqueness is that it's both . . . and. All the points of contact between these two worlds trace the way my garden has been a large part of my spiritual practice and awareness, and how I hope to inspire you.

Beginning gardeners often don't know how or where to begin. Even many experienced ones have gardens that are "nice" but lack soul. By the time you finish this book, I hope you will develop the part of yourself that is able to see the world through different eyes—to start fresh in each new moment.

Of course, I will also share with you practical information to aid you as you create your own special garden—one that is beautiful, unique, and a reflection of yourself and the values you cherish. But to accomplish that, you must first be willing to get in touch with your own inner beauty.

I believe that gardening and devotional practices are one and the same. They are expressions that spring from shared roots. At the end of each chapter, we will explore these practices in a section called "Bringing It Home." You will find garden practices as well as spiritual practices. Garden practices will help you create your physical garden, while spiritual practices direct the heart and mind to focus on the Divine. You might think of these as pathways to inner peace. We will explore a variety of practices throughout the book.

Without my spiritual perspective, I would be a different person. My garden would be very different as well. Creating as the expression of one's soul brings a feeling of exhilaration. That exhilaration comes from the discovery of new ways of looking at life and one's work, along with the feeling that all things are possible. It comes from connecting to a place of inner truth.

As a soul, I seek peace—peace of mind, inner peace, ease of heart, transcendent beauty, and oneness with God. When it works, although it is not a conscious process, my garden is a manifestation of these feelings.

So, even if you find that creating a physical garden is not right for you, I hope this book helps you discover a path to your own unique inner garden, sparking your creativity and inspiring you to follow your dreams and experience the sacred quality of life. And since love is the most important thing in life, I hope this book will ultimately touch your heart.

With love and blessings,
Janaki Sandy Gaal

"The lesson I have thoroughly learnt, and wish to pass on to others, is to know the enduring happiness that the love of a garden gives."

—GERTRUDE JEKYLL

Envisioning Your Garden

Chapter One

Looking back, I had no idea how my garden would evolve—for regardless of the plans you may have, there is always an element of mystery, just like in life. A vision is helpful to start with, but Mother Nature often contributes volunteers here and there, changes in colors and growth habits, impressions of critters, and the effects of weather. I had no idea that I would eventually open my garden to the public, be featured in magazines, and that I would be invited to speak at rose societies and The Huntington Botanical Gardens. I just followed my heart and became devoted to my garden.

"A garden is a delight to the eye
and a solace for the soul."

—SAADI

Down THE *Garden Path*

I came upon the concept that a garden has a soul on a sunny spring Saturday, when 1,400 people visited my garden. People kept coming up to me and telling me how peaceful the garden felt. I couldn't believe it! I wondered, *How is it possible to feel peace when surrounded by hundreds of people?*

A garden is really a very personal place, regardless of how many people may be there at one time, and it reflects the nature of the person or people who tend it. I have learned that gardens tended with love develop a soul and the sources of this love are as numerous as the beings that visit the gardens. It wasn't until I started to explore this subject—what gives a garden a sense of *soul*—that I realized that the evolution of the soul of *my garden* is also the story of *my own* evolution.

ROOTS

We all have roots, our beginnings in life. When these roots are nourished, it allows us to blossom into good human beings. My roots, as everyone's do, began in childhood.

As a little girl, my Grandma Sonia made quite the impression on me. And before I was old enough to be conscious of knowing what a role model was, I had one. She was a spiritual woman, and long after she had lost the ability to see clearly enough to read, she would hold the Torah in her hands, reciting the words to God from memory in Hebrew.

She had lived in a small town in Saskatchewan, Canada. She was known for her abundant garden of vegetables, fruit, and flowers, which she shared with everyone. I am more like my grandma than anyone else I am related to.

Six decades later, as part of my daily spiritual practice, I pick up Tulsidas's *Ramcharitmanas*, the most devotional version of the ancient Hindu holy book the *Ramayana*, open it to a random page, and read for thoughts with which to begin my day. As for sharing the gifts from my garden, it was a constant joy. And sure enough—after a fulfilling 10 years in nursing—I turned to the garden.

My husband, Peter, and I had our first home in Pacific Palisades in Los Angeles.

Creating a garden there was a challenge because there was quite a bit of shade. Still, there was an area of sun big enough for a tiny vegetable garden. I also wanted to grow a couple of roses, so, in order to elevate them to get enough sun, I planted half a dozen roses in half whiskey barrels.

Although I loved gardening, I quickly realized I needed more knowledge. Fortunately, just at that moment, life supplied me with a gift when I met Joe Seals, the man I nicknamed my "garden guru." He was a horticultural consultant working at a nursery nearby in Santa Monica. After asking him a few plant questions over the course of several visits, I discovered that I had found a person who knew everything about plants.

Although I read every garden book I could get my hands on, my knowledge couldn't begin to compare to his. So, I kept hanging out at the nursery, and finally, I asked him to teach me everything he could. In the years that followed, he taught me everything from drafting to organic gardening and dazzled me with his incredible plant lists.

One evening, Joe invited me to a meeting of local plant lovers. These were not backyard gardeners but professional landscape architects, garden writers, rosarians (very knowledgeable rose gardeners), and garden designers—including the legendary horticulturalist Phil Chandler. The conversations were inspiring. One of the "guests" was a Bourbon rose called 'Honorine de Brabant.' She had the intense fragrance of an Old Garden Rose. It was a scent that could make you fall in love with roses forever. And that is exactly what happened to me!

ROSE ROOTS

As with people, helping roses become established by nourishing their roots is of utmost importance. When planting a bare-root rose—young plants that have had their roots cut back and removed from the earth to be transplanted in new soil—the importance of how to dig a proper hole is always emphasized:

- Dig a generous hole to allow space for roots to grow and flourish.
- Turn and soften the soil so when the tender roots begin to grow, they can do so freely and easily.
- Provide the proper nourishment and water.
- Protect the rose from the elements of weather, insects, and disease.
- Guide the rose's growth by attentively deadheading and pruning.

As with raising a child, it is so gratifying to watch roses grow and blossom. They respond to our loving care and attention by manifesting fully. But if their root systems aren't tended carefully, they will struggle until they hopefully find their own way.

I soon joined the Pacific Palisades Garden Club (PPGC) and became its youngest member. It was wonderful to meet other gardeners—mostly couples in their 70s and 80s. Many of them became dear friends and surrogate grandparents. A positive outlook, youthful energy, and their lack of focus on any physical issues or limitations were pearls of life I saw modeled before me.

My little garden was included in one of the annual PPGC Garden Tours. With the encouragement of my garden club "family," and under Joe's guidance, I started designing gardens. I did everything myself—design, purchase, and installation—and I loved it! I devoted myself to gardening and became a garden designer.

And then we had the opportunity to move out to the country. It took me about nine months to find a house in Santa Paula, about eight miles inland from Ventura—the cute beach town we used to drive through to get to Santa Barbara and Northern California. The funny thing was that the house we ended up buying was one of the first my realtor took me to see. At first, I couldn't really see its potential. After looking endlessly, my realtor urged me to take a second look at the farm property. And this time, as we approached, she taught me a very valuable lesson. She said, "Don't see it as it is. Imagine it the way you would dream it could be." (This works well with creative projects, though I do not recommend it for relationships!)

Things often don't turn out as you imagine. Sometimes they are even better. Often it is the little choices that make a big difference. Now, I have faith. Receiving the grace of experiences I never imagined, I have surrendered to not knowing and having that faith. I have learned not to invest so much in the outcome that you can't enjoy the process. Trust, have faith, pay attention, and be open.

"The roots of all living things are tied together. Deep in the ground of being, they tangle and embrace. If we look deeply, we find that we do not have a separate self-identity, a self that does not include sun and wind, earth and water, creatures and plants, and one another."

—ROSHI JOAN HALIFAX

Gaals' LITTLE *Acre*

Never in my wildest dreams did I imagine that one day I would have a home in the country, with a space to raise a family, grow my own food, manifest my love of roses, create a little farm complete with animals—and to do so in partnership with Mother Nature and an incredible husband. It was a place that would be a refuge for all.

Peter, a dedicated cardiovascular surgeon, had never been interested in gardening. But when it was reframed as farming, all of a sudden he developed new interest. And the addition of a shiny red rototiller with a chipper/shredder attachment made it even more fun. Sometimes we need to change our perception of how we label things in order to fully appreciate them.

Our little acre had an orchard—which was home to 42 orange and 24 avocado trees. We were such amateur farmers that we could not figure out why all those beautiful avocados weren't getting ripe. We didn't know that avocados don't ripen on the trees. You have to pick them!

There were also individual trees of many other varieties—apple, peach, a young mango, papaya, sapote, quince, walnut, pomegranate, persimmon, cherimoya, and a gigantic old macadamia nut tree. There were a few clumps of bananas, too, and even a small patch of sugarcane.

After our first crop of blackberries, Peter became the keeper of the berry vines. This led to an interest in canning the most delicious blackberry jam (recipe on page 148!) and to the pruning of our fruit trees.

We both began to do research on all the crops we had inherited, which soil amendments and fertilizers were needed (although the native soil was rich and wonderful), and how to prune fruit trees. I started reading everything I could about roses and joined the Ventura County Rose Society.

One of Peter's hobbies was carpentry. He was so happy to have before him an endless assortment of wonderful creative projects. His garage became his workshop—his sacred space—where he built a variety of useful things to have on a farm. He also rototilled an area at the far end of our little acre, which was in full sun, and I planted my first real veggie garden.

The First Rose Planted

· Soulful Sanctuaries ·

THE TRANSFORMATION

Even before the veggie garden, the first thing I planted was a rose. And not just any rose—I planted a climbing (cl.) 'Cecile Brunner,' also known as "The Sweetheart Rose," centered against the front of the house. In a short amount of time, she adorned the wall, giving it the look of an English country home, just as I had hoped for and imagined.

And then I went about removing everything that did not blend with my vision. I envisioned—and, little by little, created—a classic English border with perennials, annuals, and a few roses. At some point in our early years at Gaals' Little Acre, I planted Boston ivy around most of the house. In no time at all, we had an ivy-covered cottage, finishing the charming English country garden look that I so loved.

'Cecile Brunner' (Cl. Polyantha, 1881), many years after its first planting, adorning the White Garden—the garden we planted near the front of the house. It was inspired by the world-famous White Garden at Sissinghurst Castle, designed by Vita Sackville-West in the 1930s in Kent, England.

The Orchard

Soulful Sanctuaries

The orchard ended up being the largest garden at Gaals' Little Acre. But in those early years, when the orchard was still only an orchard, one of the Valencia orange trees died, about three trees back from the center row. Once we removed it, suddenly, I was able to see exciting new possibilities. Because of this new vision, I had two more orange trees removed, creating a large open space in full sun. This area evolved into another beautiful veggie garden, and later, I was inspired to create a potager—a French kitchen garden. Potagers often have a certain formality, and mine had boxwood parterres, veggies, herbs, roses, ornamentals, and an espaliered apple tree. In dealing with change or creating change, whether it is in the worldly arena or spiritually, sometimes we cannot visualize the possibilities until the time is right . . . or is it ripe?

RIGHT: Early map of Orchard Rose Garden by Nick Williams. OPPOSITE, TOP, LEFT: We called this area of the Orchard Garden "Media Lunas" (Spanish for half-moons). This also included rustic structures made by my gardeners for growing sugar snap peas, string beans, and cucumbers. OPPOSITE, TOP RIGHT, and BOTTOM: The early days of the Orchard Garden as it grew and expanded.

TOP, RIGHT: Several years after first planting, here is 'Cl. Pinkie' (Climber, 1952) in full bloom.

VISIONARY VEGGIES

Early in our relationship, Peter took me to a workshop at the Esalen Institute in Big Sur. Esalen was the central force in the Human Potential Movement, started in the 1960s. The encounter groups, led by a variety of brilliant, compassionate minds, encouraged the exploration and growth of inner psychological and spiritual worlds. It was a movement that fostered the expansion of consciousness in general.

Esalen is also known for its awesomely beautiful, extremely productive organic vegetable gardens, which are set against the incomparable backdrop of the Big Sur coast. These gardens were the inspiration that came to mind when planting my first big vegetable garden.

My GARDENING *Philosophy*

My gardening philosophy exists on many levels, and as I attempted to define those levels here, an image of an onion with all its layers came to mind.

The outermost layer of my onion is my understanding that life in the garden works as a metaphor for life in general. For example, there is conception and birth—the planting of a seed that sprouts. With time, protection, nourishment, and love, that seed will grow into whatever it is meant to be. During its life it will experience good weather and bad, thorns, weeds, predators, disease, and perhaps even accidents.

Across every season, there is aging and change, more realized to me now as I witness many friends suffering with various health issues. In the garden, many plants turn colors and drop their leaves. The leaves are actually dying, but before they die, they become very beautiful. For example, the Boston ivy that covered much of our house was breathtakingly beautiful in the fall. Then, like people, the plants change form and drop their bodies, yet their souls remain. Some are composted and nourish new growth. Some are deciduous and will come to life again. And some others have finished their work and move on. An interesting phenomenon is that the change in color of the leaves is produced by a decrease in chlorophyll, which is caused by the onset of cold weather. The potential for aging and death is always present, but only at the appointed time is that actualized.

The second layer of my onion is an intellectual one—a mind that learns all it can about what it takes to create a garden. I was fortunate to have a garden guru who knew everything there is to know about plants. I strongly encourage you to learn all you can about gardening. Pay attention to detail.

The third layer of my onion is a feeling of peace—a precious sense of inner peace. When you are totally focused, totally in the moment, there is peace. And gardening takes you there. However, it can be difficult to feel that sense of peace and be fully present when you are responsible for the care of the garden and constantly noting what needs to be done. One method that allows me to have a more meditative feeling while in my garden is organization.

I prefer using a physical notebook over a computer. But by having a system that works for me, I don't need to remember endless details.

The fourth layer of my onion is creativity. Some people are just naturally creative; others have to work at it. It does help to quiet down and get in touch with your more intuitive side. It takes time and patience and looking with different eyes. I love this statement by Ram Dass: "Creativity springs from the yearning to be the fullness of who you are." Although my garden began in that spirit, it evolved into an expression of love for the Divine and a desire to share that love with others. My advice is to always create your garden in a way that is meaningful to you.

The fifth layer of my onion is my belief that I am but a steward of this land, working alongside Mother Nature and the forces of the Universe to nurture the earth and create beauty.

The innermost layer, at the center of my philosophical onion and my life, is a love of God. Being knowledgeable about roses is an excellent vehicle for being with people and sharing spirit. I feel God's presence in my garden and especially in my roses. I hope that what I share with people is that feeling (in addition to how to get rid of aphids organically, of course).

All in all, for me, gardening is a spiritual experience. I cannot help but be fully present. As I experience the moment, time becomes timeless, and I am filled with that peaceful sense of feeling at one with nature.

GARDEN MAINTENANCE

- Make garden rounds regularly, noting what your garden needs. I have a monthly calendar of garden jobs specific to my garden and many, many lists. Things like fertilizing schedules, seed lists, rose lists, favorite plants and combinations, integrated pest management, and pruning schedules are all tracked in my notebooks.
- Keep it clean. Your garden will be happier and healthier.
- Nip it in the bud. Take care of problems in the garden when you first spot them. It's easy to say, "Oh, there's just a few mealybugs," and do nothing about it. But before you know it, they will have taken over your plant.

BRINGING IT HOME

Garden Practice

GET READY TO CREATE YOUR OWN GARDEN

Being in a garden is an emotional experience and a delight for all the senses. My inspiration for gardening is love—love of beauty and spirit. My garden reflects the things I love and value.

When you design your garden, include what you love—what evokes joy, what turns you on. If you have a family or animals, of course consider their needs and safety. I believe if your garden brings you joy, those visiting your garden will feel that.

Everyone has a garden within them. To get started discovering yours, gather together information and experiences to inspire and educate you:

- Visit public and private gardens and nurseries—in your own area and wherever you might travel. This will give you a visual for the potential size of the different plants you hope to include.
- Read everything of interest to you about gardens—books, magazines, and garden journals.
- Take or save photos of garden ideas that appeal to you. Create a file of "Gardens I Love" and pull them out when planning your garden.
- When you see something you like, whether it is a particular combination of plants or colors—or a rose you fall in love with—make a note of it.
- Learn all about the requirements for the different plants you like.
- Perhaps you can join a local garden club or rose society.

LEFT: My beloved Puli (Hungarian sheepdog), Rami, guarding the roses I just cut.

GOING TO THE NURSERY

The nursery: a place where our human babies are nurtured and baby plants are grown for our gardens. Before going to the nursery, know the area where you want to plant. If you have a firm idea of what you would like to plant, it is possible to have the nursery order exactly what you have in mind. I usually prefer an approach that is more casual, creative, and my kind of fun. That approach means going to the nursery, seeing what looks good and will fit in the area you want to plant, and—like an artist with a whole palette of colors and textures—selecting your plants to paint a beautiful garden.

This is the time to close your eyes, dream, and visualize. Spend time in the intended site of your garden. Take careful note of the light—sunny areas, shady areas—at different times of the day. Listen to what the garden tells you.

While envisioning your garden, you might want to consider these elements that help create charm and evoke spiritual feelings in the garden:

❀ *Signs with meaningful sayings:* One of my favorite garden signs says, "This is a garden of memories, walk quietly and lift your heart to God."

❀ *Topiaries,* for a touch of whimsy.

❀ *Statues* can evoke the feelings you want represented in your garden. I like to use statues of Buddha, who brings to mind compassion and wisdom. They remind me to stop, breathe, and quiet down.

❀ *Places for birds to visit:* Try adding birdhouses, feeders, or a birdbath.

❀ *Fountains* bring in the peaceful sound of the water element.

❀ *Theme gardens* are a fun way to organize your garden.

Also, realize that gardens come in all sizes. I used to have a large, amazing garden. Now I have a tiny garden and grow only a few roses, veggies, and herbs in containers. It is the love and attention you give your garden that will give it soul and nourish you. So, do what you can and make it special. A small, simple garden is a beautiful thing.

See page 212 for more pearls of garden design. Then, take a pencil and sketch out the possibilities for your garden. Remember, though, things rarely turn out as you imagined. Allow for spontaneity.

BRINGING IT HOME

Spiritual Practice

Spirituality is a state of mind. It is feeling the presence of the Divine in everything and everyone.

There are many forms of spiritual practice—ways of relating from your soul rather than from your ego and mind. These are practices that direct the heart and mind to focus on the Divine. You might think of these as pathways to inner peace.

PRACTICE MINDFULNESS

Mindfulness is being fully present in the moment. It is listening deeply, letting go of your agenda, having compassion, and living from your soul. It is being here now.

Ram Dass taught that before you can do inner spiritual work, you first must "quiet your mind and open your heart." I feel the same is true of the creative process. I believe imagination requires timeless periods of being and puttering in the garden—listening within, visualizing, and dreaming. Sometimes just taking time for silence is all that is necessary to get you in touch with your creativity.

And as for opening your heart—at the center of everything is learning to love. Just start with what you love most—your family, your dog, your roses—and expand from there.

"The first step toward not being unconsciously influenced by something is to become conscious of it."

—RAM DASS

"The best form in which to worship God is in all forms."

—NEEM KAROLI BABA "MAHARAJ-JI"

PRACTICE MANTRA

Mantras are sacred names, sounds, phrases, or prayers that are repeated over and over as reminders of and expressions of devotion to God, in whatever way that manifests for you. The word *mantra* means "mind protecting." Once you are established in this practice, it is very centering and helps transform your consciousness. You do this by repeating your mantra as often as possible, either silently, aloud, or in song.

When your mantra becomes part of you and you experience things like fear, anxiety, pain, or anger, you naturally will remember and repeat your mantra and become centered. Mantras can be practiced with or without using a *mala*, or prayer beads. Just the feeling of the mala passing through your fingers can be centering. I actually sleep with a mala in my hand.

I invite you to choose a mantra that speaks to your spiritual heart.

CREATE A PUJA TABLE

Puja means "prayer". Puja can be performed at a table, in your garden, or in a room that is devoted to spiritual practice, as well as in the silence of your own heart.

In your home, this is your sacred space. You will want to make it beautiful. You can cover the table with a cloth. Place photos of loved ones and, images or statues of holy beings. Offering flowers to your beloved is a sweet form of devotion and expression of love. Make this a sanctuary—a holy space, set apart from the world. Have a place to sit before your sacred space—a space for meditation, reflection, prayer, or reading spiritual books. Add a candle and incense and enjoy.

SAMPLE MANTRAS

From the Hindu tradition:
Sri Ram Jai Ram Jai Jai Ram.
"Beloved Ram, I honor you."

From the Buddhist tradition:
Om mani padme hum.
"I bow to the jewel in the lotus of the heart."

From the Christian tradition:
"Our Father, who art in heaven, hallowed be thy name."

Sufi Path of the Heart:
Sufis are mystics within the religion of Islam—a path of the heart, seeking the dissolution of one's ego and a merging into God (Allah). Their practice focuses on loving, remembering, and surrendering to God. Sufis have sacred phrases called *wazaif* instead of mantras. They are known as the beautiful 99 names of Allah. Primary are Bismillah, Ya Rahman, Ya Raheem. This translates as opening to and calling on compassion and mercy.

A sacred Jewish prayer:
Shema Yisrael, Adonai Eloheinu Adonai Echad.
"Hear O Israel, the Lord our God, the Lord is One."

Sacred sounds:
Om is considered to be the sound of the Universe. It has been expressed as "In the beginning was the word, and the word was God." (John 1:1)

Ancient Sanskrit prayer:
Lokah Samastah Sukhino Bhavantu.
"May all beings everywhere be happy and free, and may the thoughts, words, and actions of my own life contribute in some way to that happiness and to that freedom for all."

From The Garden To The Kitchen

CHOCOLATE CHIP BUNDT CAKE
with Fresh Roses

This cake is great on its own or served with vanilla ice cream;
believe it or not, it's also good for breakfast.
Sometimes I use a Bundt pan shaped like a rose.

1¼ cups plus 1 teaspoon sugar

½ cup (1 stick) butter, at room temperature

1 teaspoon vanilla extract

2 eggs, beaten

1 cup sour cream or plain yogurt

2 cups all-purpose flour

1 teaspoon baking powder

½ teaspoon baking soda

8 ounces dark chocolate chips

2 teaspoons ground cinnamon

1 teaspoon sugar

Fresh organic roses and other edible flowers, to decorate the cake and platter

MAKES 1 BUNDT CAKES

1. Preheat the oven to 350°F. Grease and flour a 9- or 10-inch Bundt pan and set aside.
2. In the bowl of a stand mixer or in a large bowl with an electric mixer, beat the sugar and butter on medium speed until well combined, about 1 minute.
3. Add the vanilla, eggs, and sour cream and beat well.
4. In a medium bowl, combine the flour, baking powder, and baking soda.
5. Add the flour mixture to the sugar mixture and beat until well combined. Fold in the chocolate chips.
6. Pour half the batter into the prepared Bundt pan. In a small bowl, mix together the cinnamon and sugar. Sprinkle the mixture over the batter. Pour in the remaining batter.
7. Bake for 45 minutes, or until a toothpick inserted into the cake comes out clean. Let the cake cool in the pan for 1 hour. Remove the cake from the pan and let cool completely.
8. Place the cake on a platter and decorate with fresh roses.

Amazing Grace

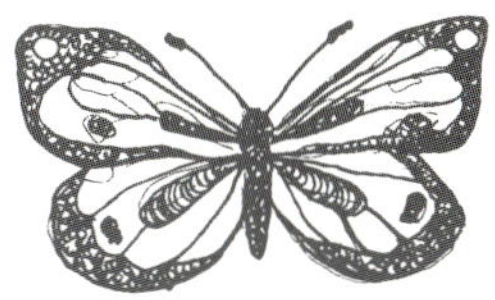

CHAPTER TWO

Everyone is looking for meaning in their lives. As you may have noticed by now, I see the garden as a metaphor for human life. We all know what a garden is. But many are not aware that within each of us dwells an inner garden—the unspoken, unmanifest form of the one spirit. This is *the heart center*. The soul resides there and it is where the inner garden blooms. The cycles in nature and within our own being mirror each other. Soul is infused throughout.

"Gardening is a gentle act."

—BEATRIX FARRAND

THE *Path* TO THE *Inner Garden*

When my heart is filled with love, what better way to share these feelings with others than by manifesting beauty, joy, and love in the creation of a garden? It's a funny thing, but in creating or maintaining a garden, you are also nourishing yourself—it's just a good thing all around. As I cultivate the spiritual heart of my garden, it nurtures my own. Like the physical garden, the inner garden—the garden of my spiritual heart, or soul—is born of love.

GARDEN AS A TEACHING

Gardening is a hobby or practice that nourishes body, mind, and spirit. It keeps you grounded and centered, mindful and present, allowing you to connect with the world of nature and expand into something greater than yourself.

Gardening is therapeutic. In addition to providing fresh air, sunshine, vitamin D, endorphins, and a creative outlet, gardening improves one's quality of life, decreases the stress hormone cortisol, and helps lower blood pressure. In people with depression or anxiety, gardening can replace these feelings with a sense of accomplishment, joy, peace, and wonder. It brings you firmly into the moment. I feel that this one-pointed presence is the true source of gardening's therapeutic power..

The teachings and gifts that a garden offers can guide your life, offer joy and comfort, and even provide you with your own food. If children have a connection to a garden, it can benefit them throughout their lives and be a happy memory from childhood.

Of course, gardening is also a lot of hard work! But if you put love into your garden, you receive even more in return—that warm inner feeling that you have done something fundamentally good and meaningful.

THE GARDEN TEACHES MANY OF LIFE'S MOST IMPORTANT LESSONS:

- nurturing
- patience
- discovering a sense of hope and wonder
- gratitude
- love
- devotion
- respect for the needs of a variety of beings
- learning to trust one's intuition
- appreciating the changes of the seasons
- working as part of a team
- educating yourself to accomplish your goals
- learning the work ethic of "reaping what you sow"
- the importance of persevering
- sharing
- taking pride in your accomplishments
- appreciating beauty
- compassion
- the transient nature of everything
- the inevitability of death and rebirth

OPPOSITE, TOP: A view of our French Rose Garden in honor of visits from Jean-Pierre Guillot. At the top of the photo, you can see the Secret Garden, and beyond that, the '60s Peace Garden.

TENDING YOUR INNER GARDEN

Without adequate "inner gardening," it is difficult to see inner beauty. When we nurture our inner garden, the soul shines through levels of personality and ego. It is luminous and radiant. If we don't go inside, make space, prune, weed, and clean up, it will become neglected, overgrown, and in need of love. The neglect can show up physically as illness, weight gain or loss, poor eating habits, sluggishness, poor physical hygiene, emotional imbalance, or an inability to finish work or projects.

If you feel your inner garden is neglected, take out the dead matter by the roots. Clear away small stuff on your own and get help with the "trees" (things you can't do by yourself). Prune what has gotten out of hand.

Create and design a new garden for the next phase of your life. Boundaries create order out of chaos. Fences and gates keep dogs or deer out of physical gardens, and often boundaries are necessary in relationships, too.

If you are not happy in your garden of the heart, weed it. And just as you provide room for seating, make room (with time and solitude) in the inner garden of your life to just be. There is wisdom that is hidden in every ordinary life.

For most of us who lead busy lives, it is necessary to quiet our minds in order to connect with our inner selves. Of course, one of the best ways to quiet the mind is meditation. (See page 85 for a guided one to try.) Many of us who garden, however, are familiar with another type of meditation—tending a garden.

It is primarily through spiritual practices that we nurture the sanctuary of our inner garden.

THE *Joy* OF *Gardening*

I remember when my love of gardening began. I got my driver's license the day I turned 16, and one of the first places I drove to was an indoor plant shop several miles away. I was curious about it, because even from the outside it looked like a jungle. Once I went inside, I discovered it felt like a jungle, too.

It was warm and humid. It smelled earthy and clean. And it was filled with all types of healthy, thriving plants. For me, it was a whole new world. I read the names of the plants and it was like meeting new friends. I bought a plant book so that I could learn more. I also bought my first plant—a four-inch philodendron—which I nurtured devotedly. It went all the way through college with me.

There's a certain magic and naïveté involved in gardening. It's not necessary to take a course in botany to be a gardener, though I do feel it is important to become knowledgeable about what you are responsible for caring for.

But still, there is something magical about planting a bare root—just some sticks with thorns—and growing a beautiful rosebush. On my early morning strolls, it is such a delight to discover a new flower in bloom that wasn't there yesterday. When you are intimately involved with your garden, you notice each new leaf and flower, and always, it is nothing less than a miracle.

Really, gardening is quite an intimate affair when you stop to think about it. There is the planting of seeds and the nurturing of life. And every evening, when I walk through my garden to say goodnight, it feels like leaving the world behind and going to meet a lover.

Nikki, our beloved golden retriever. We had two golden retrievers that we lovingly referred to as our bookends because they went everywhere with us, each on one side or the other.

Spiritual Roots

Devotion is cultivated in many ways. Just as the evolution of a garden is intimately connected to that of the gardener, my spiritual evolution was and is intimately connected to the events of my life. I followed my heart, which has proven to be such a beautiful choice.

I wasn't looking for a guru. I barely knew anything about spiritual teachers. But it was that incomparable era of the 1960s, and I was living in San Francisco—talk about being in the right place at the right time! It was a time of hippies, flower children, innocence and incense, idealism, and a free-flowing spirit of love. It was all reflected in the bohemian style of dress, the far-out language and gatherings, such as "love-ins" and "be-ins"—usually held in Golden Gate Park—and concerts with strobe lights and great music. It was a time of acknowledgment—of sexuality, homosexuality, and the equality of women and people of color. It was a time of the Vietnam War and political unrest. It was a time of consciousness-raising in general. It was an exciting time!

And yes, there were drugs—an abundance of marijuana and psychedelics, particularly LSD. But I was a student nurse in my early 20s from a fairly traditional background and living away from home for the first time. I watched the "be-ins" and the "love-ins" in Golden Gate Park from the outside. I loved the incredible, free-spirited energy of the whole scene, but I was stuck in my separateness, and at that point, could only enjoy it all vicariously.

They say that if you remember the '60s, you weren't really there. But I remember that first time I heard Ram Dass speak. A dear friend had heard about a new, "far-out" spiritual teacher and invited me to go hear a lecture by Baba Ram Dass called "One Man's Journey to the East." It was June of 1969. To tell you the truth, I don't even remember what he said. But it touched my heart and soul, and I was drawn to him with an unexplainable intensity. It was far beyond being in love—it was not romantic. It was the love of a soul who spoke to my soul—a level of being I was not previously even aware of. Ram Dass was another being giving words to my innermost feelings, evoking the yearning for and love of God.

The soul connection I've shared with Ram Dass for more than five decades years has been exquisitely beautiful. For me, he is my beloved spiritual teacher (he does not like to be called a guru) and my dearest friend. He gave words to the feelings that lay undiscovered in my heart of hearts. In gardening terms, there were seeds that lay dormant in my *hridayam* (Sanskrit for "spiritual heart"). He came along and watered them, creating forevermore the most awesome garden—the garden of the heart, which flourishes with a love of God. That love manifests as a love of the spirit present in all beings—a love of nature, beauty, and life. It is a relationship based on truth and love and devotion to God. It is a relationship that has allowed me to know my soul.

"Your mind is a garden. Your thoughts are the seeds. The harvest can either be flowers or weeds."

—WILLIAM WORDSWORTH

TOP: Part of the greenhouse.

BRINGING IT HOME

Garden Practice

CONNECTING THE INNER AND OUTER GARDENS: ORGANIC GARDENING

The visible and invisible worlds are intertwined: the outer and inner gardens. The inner garden is a reflection of how we take care of our lives, bodies, minds, spirits, and soul. That inner spirit feeds life in the world. The garden and everything you do then becomes an expression or reflection of your inner work. To take care of the earth is a spiritual practice as well as a garden practice. Awareness and connectedness to the earth give us joy. Organic gardening is one important way to honor Mother Earth and care for both the inner and outer gardens. After all, caring for the earth feels good!

I became an advocate of organic gardening long before it was popular. As a new RN in the early '70s, I was working at UCLA on a medical floor. Many of my patients had leukemia and lymphoma, and many of them were gardeners or farmers who had excessive exposure to pesticides and herbicides. Sadly, many of them died. Treatments have gotten better since then, but dangerous pesticides are still widely in use today.

Then, when my daughter, Becky, was about two years old, I joined a local group called Mothers and Others for Safe Food. That group was part of a national organization started by the actress Meryl Streep, who was motivated by the Alar apple scare. Alar was a plant-growth regulator that left a residue both in apple juice and applesauce—food basic to the diets of babies and young children. The residue was thought to be toxic at the time. I had this precious baby, and I wanted to do everything I could to protect her, so my involvement with the group was natural. The purpose of the group was to increase public awareness of organic gardening and the health hazards of pesticides. In the late 1980s, the only place in the U.S. where you could buy organic produce was at a health food store—and that produce was small, often disfigured, and overpriced. Farmers' markets were just starting to become popular. Now, some 40 years later, an abundance of beautiful organic produce is available at local supermarkets. Farmers' markets have become a popular weekly ritual for many of us.

Although the general awareness of organic gardening has greatly increased and improved, for those of us who garden organically, it is not always easy because we seem to be going against convention. No matter what the subject, when your feelings or beliefs are different from most people around you, it requires deep conviction to follow your heart and do what you believe in. Or, as Shakespeare wrote, "To thine own self be true." It is worth the effort because not doing what you truly believe in causes a lack of inner harmony. And the older I get, the more precious that sense of inner peace becomes!

I consider the three basic reasons to garden organically to be:

1. To promote good health for oneself and one's family.
2. To honor our Mother Earth by not polluting the environment.
3. To follow the horticulturally correct way to garden—a natural, organic way—rather than, using chemical pesticides and herbicides.

As you work to plant an organic veggie or herb garden, I invite you to pay attention to two principles of organic gardening.

The first is this: No use of chemical fertilizers, pesticides, or herbicides. I recently read an interesting statistic: In 2017, the USGS reported that the U.S. uses about one billion pounds of pesticides each year. As of 2023, the United Nations reported that the United States is still second only to China in its pesticide use. Endangering birds, wildlife, and water is way too high a price for a perfect rose—not to mention polluting our Mother Earth or endangering our health and well-being. For alternatives to using pesticides, see my suggestions for pest, disease, and weed control on page 220.

The second principle of organic gardening is this: Take care of your soil. What do you use? How do you feed the soil? When I think of organic gardening, the first thing that comes to mind is the quality of the soil. This is where seeds germinate—where life begins. That's why we call it Mother Earth!

In creating my gardens, I used the Biodynamic French Intensive method of organic gardening. The proponents of this method were Alan Chadwick, John Jeavons, and J. I. Rodale. It involves creating raised beds in the ground by double digging the soil and incorporating compost and other organic amendments to aerate and improve the quality of the soil.

Crops are planted close together, creating an increased yield and leaving no room for weeds to grow. Biodynamic gardening also uses the practices of crop rotation, companion planting, and composting. This sustainable form of organic gardening is what I credit for the health and beauty of my gardens. At times I also consulted the wisdom of *The Old Farmer's Almanac*—especially for ideal times to plant seeds. (For example, planting during a full moon will help seeds germinate faster because of the stronger gravitational pull.) For more information on companion planting, see page 222.

COMPOST!

The best way to take care of your soil is by using compost. Remember that the purpose of compost is to improve the structure of the soil, thereby increasing resistance to disease and promoting healthy growth. Good compost is exciting to the garden and the gardener alike.

It's a good idea to keep a small bucket or container near the kitchen sink for fruit and vegetable scraps, coffee grounds, and eggshells you would otherwise throw away. Do not add anything oily. Adding materials regularly will keep your compost from getting moldy and therefore unusable.

You may also add garden trimmings that have not gone to seed and healthy grass cuttings. It's important not to add dog or cat poop or any diseased garden clippings. Also, I learned the hard way that if you want to add chicken manure to your compost, you need to find a way to separate that from chicken feed on the ground. I ended up with a lot of corn seedlings in various parts of the garden.

Compost bins or piles should be located in full sun, regularly turned, and stored in a container that is well-aerated. Fortunately for me, Peter enjoyed building compost bins and we placed them at both ends of the garden. This facilitated loading the wheelbarrow with compost to amend the soil in spring and autumn when we prepared the beds for planting. However you decide to do it, compost will enrich your garden in so many ways!

BELOW: Our compost bin with a honeysuckle backdrop and wire sides to allow for aeration.

"The ground's generosity takes in our compost and grows beauty. Try to be more like the ground."

—RUMI

BRINGING IT HOME

Spiritual Practice

OFFERINGS FROM THE GARDEN

There is joy in sharing your garden and its gifts with others, knowing it will bring a smile to their faces. Flowers are the perfect embodiment of inner peace and beauty. They, especially roses, are messengers of love. Few things make me happier than offering a bouquet of roses from my garden.

When Peter and I moved to our acre of land, with the blessing of this newly acquired karma, feeding everybody became so easy. Because we grew a large variety of organic fruit, veggies, herbs, and flowers—and canned and baked with what we grew—it was rare that anyone who visited left empty-handed. It was also common for me to leave the house, taking the fruits of the garden to share.

Roses feed people, too. They are food for the soul. What you are given in life becomes your spiritual path. Flowers are the perfect expression of and response to both the joys and sorrows of life. We offer them in times of celebration and in times of illness and grief. Whatever the occasion, they uplift the spirits and help us deal with adversity.

I invite you—with love in your heart—to offer a flower or food you have grown to a beloved or a photo of them at your altar, or to someone in need—wherever your heart leads you.

When you have a garden that provides you with something to share, this offering becomes a wonderful, ongoing sharing of your heart.

CULTIVATE THE WITNESS

One method of becoming more mindful—more conscious—is to cultivate the witness. In the book *Polishing the Mirror*, Ram Dass explains: "The witness is actually another level of Consciousness. The witness coexists alongside your normal consciousness as another layer of awareness, as the part of you that is awakening."

The witness is an objective, non-judgmental space within, helping you become aware of and guide your feelings and behavior. You might think of the witness as your intuitive heart or inner guru. It is a place you can trust.

"Feed everybody."

—NEEM KAROLI BABA
"MAHARAJ-JI"

Peace

TAKE TIME TO REFLECT: KEEP A JOURNAL

The value of introspection and reflection is made clear in Socrates's statement that "the unexamined life is not worth living." Writing in a journal is another way of getting in touch with what is going on inside, another way of witnessing your inner life. See your life through the eyes of your soul—no judging, just noticing.

Take a look at what you need to further your spiritual growth. What are your longings? What brings you joy? How have you grown? What do you need? What serves the highest purpose? What do you add to the world? Listen to your own inner voice and learn to trust it. Have compassion for yourself.

Occasionally I will discover an old journal and just flip through it. My earliest ones seem like they were written by someone else. I noticed my innocence and my pure spiritual longings.

STUDY THE LIVES OF SAINTS

There is so much wisdom to be learned from studying the lives of saints of all faiths. Ram Dass's spiritual roots traced back to India and the spiritual saint Neem Karoli Baba, affectionately known as "Baba" or "Maharaj-ji," which means "Great King." Maharaj-ji was a manifestation of unconditional love. His love is so great that it transforms the lives of all who have the privilege of knowing him. Before meeting Maharaj-ji, Harvard professor Dr. Richard Alpert went to India. He returned, transformed, to America as the spiritual teacher Ram Dass, which means "Servant of God." Sharing Maharaj-ji's grace and his own wisdom, Ram Dass inspired several generations worldwide to an expanded, conscious, loving awareness.

KIRTAN: HINDU DEVOTIONAL SINGING

Kirtan, or Hindu devotional singing, is a form of bhakti yoga—the path of the heart. It is the yoga of devotion. The Indian saint Swami Ramdas said that devotion means loving remembrance of God who is seated in the hearts of each of us. Although this is quite a personal matter, one of the best ways to open your heart to this experience is by singing.

There are many wonderful people who lead kirtan. Krishna Das is an internationally known "rock star" of kirtan. Ram Dass said, "his heart songs open the channels to God."

Singing kirtan is one of my primary spiritual practices and brings me a lot of joy and a sense of being spiritually "centered." I invite you to consider listening to or singing kirtan or other forms of spiritual music.

Zucchini BREAD 'N' BUTTER PICKLES

These pickles are especially delicious with tuna salad. Try adding a little pickle juice to tuna to cut down on mayo.

FOR THE CANNING

Canner

8 (16-ounce) Mason jars with lids and rings

Small pot, for boiling lids and rings

FOR THE PICKLES

4 quarts (16 cups) sliced zucchini

6 medium onions, sliced

3 to 4 garlic cloves (optional)

1/3 cup pickling (kosher) salt

Cracked ice

5 cups sugar

3 cups cider vinegar

2 tablespoons mustard seed

1 ½ teaspoons celery seed

1 ½ teaspoons ground turmeric

MAKES 8 (16 OUNCE) JARS

Wanting to contribute to our new community, Peter and I entered the Ventura County Fair competition for Family Farm and won first prize!

To prepare the canning jars

1. Follow the detailed General Canning Instructions on page 146.

To make the pickles

1. In a large pot, combine the zucchini, onion, garlic (if using), and salt. Cover with cracked ice. Stir well and let sit for at least 3 hours.
2. Drain the liquid completely from the zucchini. Add the sugar, vinegar, mustard seed, celery seed, and turmeric to the zucchini and mix well.
3. Pack the zucchini mixture into the sterilized jars, making sure the zucchini is covered with liquid and leaving ½-inch headspace. Wipe the rims of the jar clean with a paper towel or kitchen towel. Top with the lids and screw on the rings.
4. Return the sealed jars to the canner and bring the water to a boil over medium-high heat. Boil for 10 minutes.
5. Remove the jars from the canner and place them on kitchen towels. Listen for the pop, pop, pop, indicating your jars have properly sealed.

CHAPTER THREE

For the Love of Roses

Gaals' Little Acre in Santa Paula, California, had an ideal growing climate. Although I have grown a variety of organic fruit, veggies, herbs, and flowers over the years, my real passion is roses. I just love roses—especially Old Garden Roses (OGRs) and English Roses.

I had approximately four hundred roses in my gardens at Gaal's Little Acre. When I'm not appreciating their beauty and fragrance, deadheading, or cutting and arranging roses for my home or friends, much of my time is spent reading about roses, photographing them, visiting other gardens, and talking with other rose lovers. Isn't that all part of being in love?

"Be like a rose, wafting to all the sweet fragrance of soul goodness."

—PARAMAHANSA YOGANANDA, *Man's Eternal Quest*

I NEVER *Promised* YOU A *Rose Garden*

My love of roses grew "like corn in the night." (I never understood that phrase until I grew my own corn. You can literally see the amazing growth of a corn stalk every day.) The more I learned about roses, the more I loved them. And when I realized I could group some of them together into "theme gardens"—well, that was just too much fun.

Most of my gardens were in the style of an English cottage garden. Using the British concept of garden rooms—or separate spaces within a garden—each of my "garden rooms" had a theme. There was an orchard, a large vegetable garden, and several "theme gardens." (More on those in chapter 4!)

My husband, Peter, never promised me a rose garden, but he sure facilitated the creation of one when we started our little acre. The result has been a wonderful gift in my life. Through it, I have realized that, like love, roses make people bloom.

"The happiness of others is light for the spirit."

—RAMAYANA

'Fortune's Double Yellow' (China, 1845)

For the Love OF *Roses*

I first attended the Celebration of Old Roses in El Cerrito, California, north of Berkeley, in the early '90s. Miriam Wilkins, the organizer of this event and the founder of The Heritage Roses Group, provided all who attended with a wonderful treat: the experience of being surrounded by the roses we so loved in many forms. She was a very gracious lady and always happy to share her wealth of knowledge of Old Roses. My favorite part of that event was the enormous variety of OGRs, cut, labeled, and close enough to smell—heavenly! The Celebration of Old Roses so delighted and impressed me that I decided to organize my own rose celebration in Southern California, and I called it "For the Love of Roses."

In 1996, I offered For the Love of Roses for the first time, and our turnout for the weekend was only about a hundred people. Although I didn't have much experience with advertising, I still had faith that this was a project I wanted to succeed, so I tried again the following year.

My garden guru mentioned my garden to his friend—the garden editor for the *L.A. Times,* Bob Smaus. At that time, there was a wonderful weekly garden magazine included with the Sunday paper. After a six-page feature on my garden came out early in the spring of 1997, I opened my country-style mailbox and found it stuffed full of responses from people wanting to visit Gaals' Little Acre. I could not believe my eyes! That year, in one spring weekend, 1,400 people came to celebrate For the Love of Roses. And from that year on, we had a following of people who visited the garden every year with their family and friends.

One of the highlights for most of these celebrations was having Clair Martin, curator of roses at The Huntington Botanical Gardens, lecture about roses and answer rose questions. There was a self-conducted garden tour, with maps of the gardens and labels for each rose, telling the name of the rose, the variety, and the date of introduction. We also set up a charming gift shop in my rustic greenhouse with rose-related and gardening treasures, and we offered a catered lunch. The Ventura County Rose Society brought cut roses, for the delight of all. Rose societies usually meet monthly, and this is a fun way to meet other rose lovers and learn more about roses. Scott Klittich, who owns Otto & Sons Nursery in Fillmore, lined my driveway with five-gallon roses for sale. The driveway never looked so beautiful!

Sharing the gardens and our love of roses with hundreds of people was wonderful. I know it brought joy and inspiration to all. I discovered that while I had once felt being a nurse was the only way I could relieve suffering, bringing joy through sharing my garden was another way to be of service.

A few comments over the years stand out in my mind: One young lady shared with my husband that she had stage 4 cancer and that being in the garden had given her a deep sense of peace and connection to something beyond this realm. A friend referred to the garden as the "Disneyland of Roses." Another friend called it "The Magical Mystery Tour."

A 91-year-old man told me, "Now I can die happy!" And there were many visitors who, in spite of being surrounded by hundreds of people, experienced peace in the garden. They were all touched by the soul of the garden, which put them in touch with their own souls and therefore with the Divine.

WHY ROSES?

Even my family and closest friends often ask me why do I do this.

Simply put, it is my desire to share the beauty of the roses. I see nature's beauty as a manifestation of God, and I want to share it.

OPPOSITE PAGE: 'The Wedgewood Rose' (Cl. English, 2009). RIGHT: 'Gertrude Jekyll®' (English, 1986).

My FAVORITE *Roses*

One of the questions I am frequently asked is, what are my favorite roses? As I mentioned earlier, I am partial to OGRs and English Roses—the more fragrant or *fully double* (meaning it has 17–25 or more petals) the better. Resistance to disease is also an important factor. So, the list that follows includes roses that are beautiful, healthy, and fragrant. This is the short list. For even more favorites, see the top 10 lists from some of my favorite rosarians (page 195).

ABOVE: 'Léontine Gervais.' RIGHT: 'Celsiana.'

OLD GARDEN ROSES

An OGR used to be defined as a rose that was introduced before 1867. According to rosarian Jeri Jennings, that definition was complicated from the start, because there have always been roses that didn't fit. She explains, "A better 'rule of thumb,' and the way it's usually stated, this: An OGR is any rose of a class of roses that was introduced before 1867." So, to clarify, even though the 'Madame Ernst Calvat' below was introduced in 1888, it belongs to the Bourbon class and counts as an OGR.

- **'Madame Ernst Calvat'** (Bourbon, introduced in 1888) *12-foot climber or pillar; medium pink; repeat bloomer; deliciously fragrant.*
- **'Celsiana'** (Damask, before 1732) *4 to 6 feet; light pink; ruffled; sweet, fragrant; does best with some winter chill; onetime bloomer.*
- **'Cecile Brunner,'** "The Sweetheart Rose" (Cl. Polyantha, 1881) *12-to-20-foot climber; sweet, light pink small roses; beautiful little rosebuds; requires substantial support (like a building or pergola); repeat bloomer.*
- **'Joasine Hanet,'** "The Portland from Glendora" (Damask Perpetual, 1847) *8-to-12-foot shrub; arching canes or as a climber; small, hot pink; very fragrant.*
- **'Sydonie'** (Damask Perpetual, 1845) *3 to 5 feet; medium pin;, fragrant; delightful.*
- **'Fortune's Double Yellow'** (China, 1845) *6-to-8-foot tall and wide specimen shrub; pale shades of pink and yellow; delicate-looking, watercolor-like roses.*
- **'Mrs. RG Sharmin Crawford'** (Hybrid Perpetual, 1894) *6-to-8-foot specimen shrub; medium pink; very fragrant.*
- **'Jacques Cartier'** (Portland, 1868) *4 to 6 feet tall; medium pink; very fragrant.*
- **'Blush Noisette'** (Noisette, 1814) *6-to-8-foot-tall and wide specimen shrub; clusters of sweet, white, fragrant, small roses.*
- **'Mutabilis'** (China, Pre-1894) *4-to-8-foot-tall and wide specimen shrub; changes colors in shades of pink and yellow; charming single petals (meaning it has 4–8 petals in a single layer) resembling butterflies.*
- **'Excellenz von Schubert'** (Hybrid Musk/ Polyantha, 1909) *8-foot-wide shrub; clusters of small lavender flowers.*
- **'Cornelia'** (Hybrid Musk, 1925) *5 feet tall and wide; light pink clusters of rosettes; blooms a lot; beautiful, big specimen; plant, tree, or climber; tolerates less sun.*
- **'Rosa Banksia Banksia' a.k.a. 'White Lady Banks'** (Rambler, 1850) *12–30-foot gigantic rambling rose; must have sturdy supportsuch as a wall; clusters of small white fragrant roses mostly in spring; magnificent specimen.*
- **'Léontine Gervais'** (Rambler, 1863) *20 or more feet; soft peach; awesome spring bloom.*
- **'Autumn Damask'** (Damask, pre-1913) *5 feet tall; light pink; very double; very fragrant.*
- **'Honorine de Brabant'** (Bourbon, 1916) *5 feet tall; light pink; very double; very fragrant.*
- **'Souvenir de la Malmaison'** (Bourbon, 1843) *3–4-foot bush; white; blooms continuously; fragrant.*

MODERN ROSES

- ❀ **'Mary Rose®'** (English, 1983) *3-to-4-foot bush; pink; blooms continuously; fragrant.*
- ❀ **'Gertrude Jekyll®'** (English, 1986) *5 feet tall; deep pink; grows as a shrub with long canes that can be pegged, or as a climber; very fragrant; good flavor in rose desserts.*
- ❀ **'Tradescant'** (English, 1994) *5 to 8 feet tall; crimson.*
- ❀ **'William Shakespeare 2000™'** (English, 1994) *3 to 4 feet; crimson; blooms a lot.*
- ❀ **'Munstead Wood®'** (English, 2007) *4 feet; burgundy; very fragrant.*
- ❀ **'Eglantyne'** (English, 1994) *3 to 4 feet; pink; large roses; very fragrant.*
- ❀ **'Charles Rennie Mackintosh'** (English, 1988) *4 feet; dusty rose/lavender; blooms continuously; fragrant.*
- ❀ **'Martine Guillot®'** (Shrub, 1997) *4 feet; white; ethereal—as lovely as the lady.*
- ❀ **'Yves Piaget®'** (Hybrid Tea, 1983) *3 to 4 feet; medium pink; large peony-like blooms; very fragrant.*
- ❀ **'Medallion'** (Hybrid Tea, 1973) *6 to 7 feet; peachy; blooms a lot.*
- ❀ **'Sweet Surrender'** (Hybrid Tea, 1983) *6 to 7 feet; pink; very fragrant; sometimes has a weak neck, but very beautiful.*
- ❀ **'Frédérich Mistral'** (Hybrid Tea, 1996) *6 to 7 feet; pale pink; very double; fragrant.*
- ❀ **'Barbra Streisand'** (Hybrid Tea, 2001) *5 to 6 feet; lavender; fragrant.*
- ❀ **'Ingrid Bergman®'** (Hybrid Tea, 1984) *4 to 6 feet; red; fragrant; beautiful form; blooms a lot.*
- ❀ **'Pristine'** (Hybrid Tea, 1978) *4 to 5 feet; white/pink; fragrant; ethereal.*
- ❀ **'Lavender Pinocchio'** (Floribunda, 1952) *3 to 5 feet; lavender/tan; semi-double; unusual color.*
- ❀ **'Lavender Lassie'** (Hybrid Musk, 1960) *4 to 6 feet; lavender/pink; semi-double; charming.*
- ❀ **'Cl. Pinkie'** (Climber, 1952) *8 to 10 feet; pink; nearly thornless canes; almost always in bloom.*
- ❀ **'Compassion®'** (Cl. Hybrid Tea, 1973) *8 to 12 feet; pink blend; fragrant.*
- ❀ **'Kathleen'** (Hybrid Musk, 1922) *8 to 12 feet; light pink; charming, five-petaled roses; looks like an apple blossom.*
- ❀ **'Sally Holmes'** (Hybrid Musk Shrub, 1976) *10 to 12 feet; white with a gold center; charming; can be grown as a climber, free-standing specimen, or part of a hedge.*
- ❀ **'Thérèse Bugnet'** (Rugosa, 1950) *6 to 8 feet; deep pink.*
- ❀ **'Veilchenblau,'** "The Blue Rose" (Rambler, 1909) *10 to 15 feet; purple blossoms that fade to gray blue; fragrant; spring bloom.*
- ❀ **'Sombreuil'** (Climber, Unknown, 1940s to 1950s) *8 to 12 feet; white, fragrant.*

RIGHT: 'Compassion®'

"A single rose can be my garden . . .
A single friend, my world."

—LEO BUSCAGLIA

BRINGING IT HOME

Garden Practice

BEING IN A RELATIONSHIP WITH ROSES

Think about what it is like to love someone or something deeply. You think of your love frequently, if not all the time. You want to be with your love and make them happy. You discover those things that make your beloved feel good—you learn all you can about them. That's my relationship with roses. Knowing their name, family, habits, and needs is a necessity.

Loving deepens the game—makes life meaningful, happier, and gives you a sense of peace and joy. So, take your love of roses and go out into the world and share that love, because a true, deep love has its roots in your soul. Whether you have a love of roses, or a love of spirit, or whatever your passion may be—the essence of love is the same. If you can reside in that place in yourself, you become love and that love touches everyone you meet.

As in any good relationship, time together to honor the relationship is essential. Remember that it takes time for a garden to evolve. Help your roses be more beautiful and productive by deadheading the spent blooms and watching for signs of disease or predators. Take care of them when they are sick. Provide them with an environment that is clean and beautiful. Remember they also benefit from the companionship of other flowers. Provide places for people to sit and be with the roses. Love, honor, and cherish them.

GROWING ROSES ORGANICALLY

Growing roses organically is possible, easier than the alternative, and more environmentally and health-conscious. How do you do this?

First, choose disease-resistant roses. Next, you need to give them the best sunlight conditions possible. Most roses need at least six hours of sun—the more the better. Water them deeply and feed them twice a year.

For nutrient amendments, I feed my roses 1 cup of mixed blood and bone meal plus 2 tablespoons of wood ash (from the fireplace) twice a year. In late winter, after pruning the roses, I also add alfalfa meal and mulch. The second feeding is in June. I use only organic methods of disease and pest control. These include beneficial insects (like trichogramma wasps), Safer® products (particularly their insecticidal soap and fungicide), and *Bacillus thuringiensis* (DiPel®). (See also page 220 for more tips on how to handle pests.)

Good housekeeping is also a factor in helping your garden grow. But most important of all is your presence. Make garden rounds frequently, become knowledgeable, and learn to anticipate potential problems. I have seen recommended feeding and spraying schedules for roses (written by non-organic rosarians) that make me cringe. They suggest feeding different combinations of fertilizers weekly and weekly spraying. There is nothing worse than inhaling what you believe to be the heavenly fragrance of a beautiful rose and getting a nose full of Systemic.

You do need to tolerate a certain amount of imperfection if you grow roses organically. But at least that is real. If you find you have certain roses that are totally covered with mildew or black spot, regardless of having provided them with ideal growing conditions, then by all means, prune them with a shovel.

Gardening organically is an expression of my love of roses and a love and respect for the earth, the environment, and myself. And whether you call it a love of roses, or a love of spirit, or whatever your passion may be, the essence of love is the same. A garden created out of love has soul. That garden touches the souls of all who enter and gives them peace.

BRINGING THE GARDEN INTO YOUR HOME—DECORATING

For those of us who love gardens and flowers, it feels natural to bring these into our homes. This can show up as the actual flowers cut from your garden, bought cut flowers, or even in fabrics, tiles, dishes, art and photographs, cushions—you get the idea.

My feeling about decorating my home is much the same as my feeling about my garden. This is my refuge, my private space away from the world, a sacred space—a spiritual sanctuary. It is a place to be alone or with family and friends. So, I make it beautiful and meaningful and encourage you to do the same. A home is a treasure beyond compare, and, hopefully, a space of comfort, beauty, peace, and joy.

Kindness

BRINGING IT HOME

Spiritual Practice

YOGA, QIGONG, TAI CHI

There are many types of yoga. When people think of yoga, they commonly think of hatha yoga, the physical form of yoga. In the West, this form of yoga has become increasingly popular. Hatha yoga is based on consciously practicing asanas (physical postures) and pranayama (breathing exercises). It is a preparation for doing deeper meditative work, as it promotes a sense of well-being in body and mind.

Qigong and tai chi, like yoga, are ancient transformative practices and exercises. While they are different in origin and form, they all have some things in common: enhancing physical health, flexibility, balance, and focus; feeling grounded; relieving stress; promoting inner peace; and preparing the body for deeper spiritual work and receptivity.

My dear friend Joyanna Maria Ananda, who teaches a beautiful interwoven practice of qigong and yoga, says: "Qigong and yoga are systems that serve the body-mind, using the mastery and power of breath, qi-prana, within particular movements, to open and circulate life force in and through the systems.

In the yogic traditions, it is suggested to practice with *sthira* (steadiness) and *sukha* (ease), finding balance. Qigong follows the ancient Chinese concept of the Tao:

> *Wu Wei—effortless action:*
> In the flow with nature
> A garden
> One's breath
> To be in harmony."

As for tai chi, my friend David Barton explains it best. He says, "Tai chi is a centuries-old martial art that is a moving meditation. It relies on the practice of 'letting go' of tension and focusing your attention and is a pathway for calmness. Both in China and the U.S., classes are often held in a park."

MEDITATION

For many people, meditation is their primary spiritual practice. There are many forms of meditation from different traditions. In *Polishing the Mirror*, Ram Dass explains that, regardless of the form, "it is a basic spiritual practice for quieting the mind and getting in touch with our deeper Self . . . Meditation provides a deeper appreciation of the interrelatedness of all things and the part each person plays."

Some forms of meditation include Vipassana, a Buddhist Insight Meditation where you follow the breath to become quiet and centered; mindfulness meditation where you notice what arises, exists, and passes away; Guru Kripa (the grace of the guru); and cloud meditation, which allows you to merge with the Universe. When someone once asked Maharaj-ji how to meditate, he responded: "Meditate like Christ."

The devotee then asked, "How did Christ meditate?"

Maharaj-ji was very quiet, and after a while

a tear trickled down his face and he said, "He lost himself in love." You might try that . . .

Now let's do a guided meditation.

ROSE MEDITATION

One way of remembering to stay centered in love that I like to use is visualizing a garden in the center of your heart. During the meditation that follows, you will have the opportunity to "become" a rose, and by doing so, cultivate a deeper knowledge of it—what it needs, what's stressing it, and how it's faring. This practice will allow you to care for your roses from a place of deeper, more intuitive understanding. When we talk about having a "green thumb," isn't that what we really mean? This is an opportunity to experience how meditation can be used to reduce stress and contribute to a quieter, more peaceful mind. It will also guide you to a sacred space.

I was introduced to a form of this rose meditation many years ago at Esalen Institute in Big Sur by an extraordinary man named Harry Sloan. Harry was a dentist from New York who, after his first experience at Esalen, left his practice to become a transpersonal psychologist and lead groups at Esalen himself for many years. He was very handsome and charismatic and manifested a lightness of being.

Harry died of cancer in his mid 40s. I found out after he died that often during his illness—and especially as he neared death—he would take one rose to bed with him and be with that rose, watching it all day as its form changed. I was told he died a very peaceful death. I had the honor of planting a rose garden at Esalen in memory of Harry.

"As a rose unfolds, it is neither impatient nor distracted from its process of becoming. We are like a rose when we choose to allow our changes. As we change, there are always parts of ourselves that are resistant to go along. Often, we energize these unnourishing parts, which hold us back from where we are going. We then experience conflict, having separated ourselves from the essential core or the heart of what is emerging."

—HARRY SLOAN

Please find a comfortable position.

You might want to have a friend read this meditation to you so you can close your eyes and really focus. Or you could record it. Now, close your eyes and take three slow, deep breaths. Keeping your eyes closed during the meditation will allow you to have a deeper, more meaningful experience.

Continue breathing slowly and deeply, following your breath as it passes from your nose to your lungs and abdomen. Feel your abdomen rise with each inhalation and fall with each exhalation, just as if you were inflating a balloon. If you find thoughts entering your mind, just notice them and let them go. And gently return to following your breath.

I would like you to visualize a beautiful garden. It can be any type of garden, any size. Maybe it's your garden at home or a place you remember from your childhood. Or maybe it's the garden you've always dreamed of creating.

I would like to invite you to plant at least one rosebush in your garden.

Now, imagine there is a beautiful, winding pathway in the garden. Take some time to wander through your garden. The weather is absolutely perfect—warm, but not hot—with a very gentle breeze caressing you.

As you walk down this path, the fragrance of flowers and the happy songs of birds greet you. At the end of the path, you come to your favorite rosebush. You look upon one perfect rose, and since you have all the time in the world, you can really appreciate this rose. Appreciate its form, its color, the stage of growth in which it is manifesting, and its heavenly fragrance.

Now let's shift our perspective. Let's go from outside the rose to inside it. Let's go from experiencing the rose to becoming the rose. Become one with this rose. Feel the warm sun shining down on you. See how the sunlight enhances your color and your perfume. Feel the warmth of the sun allowing your soft, tender petals to open freely. See and feel how beautiful you truly are. Allow yourself to be fully in this moment.

Once you have touched this place inside of you, you can always come back to this place—even though the weather will change, the warm, nourishing sun will disappear, it will get cold and rainy, your perfect form will evolve, and you will one day lose your petals and die. That is the way of nature. But you have touched the essence of love inside of you, in your soul. And that part of you never dies.

Now, in preparation for coming back, I would like you to place your beautiful garden in the center of your chest. This space is called the hridayam *(spiritual heart).*

Make a plan for how you will care for this very special garden. What will you do to nourish it? You wouldn't want your garden to be overcome by weeds, so think of your frustration and anger as weeds and let them go, remembering that you won't experience these emotions unless you are holding on to how you think things should be.

Now take a last look at that beautiful rose that you have become. Promise to take good care of it—to nurture and appreciate it, and to be with it. Remember, you can always return to this beautiful garden in your heart.

When you feel ready, you may open your eyes.

From The Garden To The Kitchen

Rose Geranium POUND CAKE

This one is for the rose lovers. Rose geraniums and rosewater give this cake the taste and aroma of a beautiful rose.

10 eggs, separated

1 pound (4 sticks) butter, softened

3 cups sugar

5½ cups all-purpose flour

6 teaspoons baking powder

¾ cup milk

2 teaspoons vanilla extract

1 teaspoon grated lemon zest

3 to 4 teaspoons rosewater

About 1 dozen organic rose geranium leaves, rinsed and dried

Organic roses, for decorating

MAKES 2 BUNDT CAKES

1. Preheat the oven to 300°F. Grease and flour two 9- or 10-inch Bundt pans.
2. In a large bowl, beat the egg whites with an electric mixer on high speed for 2 minutes. Set aside.
3. In another large bowl, beat together the butter and sugar on low speed until creamy, about 4 minutes.
4. Add the egg yolks and beat until combined, about 2 minutes.
5. In a separate bowl, sift together the flour and baking powder.
6. Beat the butter and sugar for an additional 5 minutes on low speed.
7. Add ⅓ of the flour mixture to the butter and sugar mixture and beat on low speed until mixed. Add the milk and beat until smooth. Add ½ of the remaining flour mixture and beat until mixed. Add the egg whites and beat until smooth. Add the remaining flour mixture, increase the speed to medium, and beat for 5 minutes.
8. Add the vanilla, lemon zest, and rosewater and beat on medium speed for 2 minutes.
9. Pour about ¼ of the batter into each of the prepared pans. Arrange half of the rose geranium leaves over the batter in each pan. Pour the remaining batter equally into the pans. Bake for 1 hour and 15 minutes or until the center of the cake springs back when lightly pressed with fingers.
10. Let cool in the pans on a wire rack for 10 minutes. Loosen around the sides of the pan with a knife and invert the cake onto a wire rack to cool completely.
11. Place the cake on a platter and decorate with fresh, organic roses.

Cultivating Sacred Spaces

Chapter Four

The garden has a soul that mirrors and nourishes our own. Among the many reasons gardening captivates our hearts and souls is because it is a joyful act of creativity. There is an amazing art to creating beauty in the garden—imagining what a piece of earth might look like and what it might yield and working to turn that into reality.

"In looking outward to a beautiful flower, our eye is delighted, but we are also touched inside our hearts, as Nature is a direct expression of the divine."

—ELIZABETH MURRAY, *Cultivating Sacred Spaces*

WHY *Gardening* CAPTIVATES OUR *Hearts*

In that creative process, we tap into our inner child. Creating a garden is exciting and fun. There is a childlike sense of wonder in planting seeds or bulbs or bare-root roses and watching their growth. There is a simple pleasure and deep satisfaction that comes from nurturing a garden, watering and feeding it, and watching it manifest fully—the magic of going into the garden and picking a sugar snap pea and eating it right next to the vine it grew on. Or peeling back the husks of an ear of corn, revealing the unique beauty within. Or picking an orange or apple from a tree and eating it right there in the garden. And sharing your harvest with your dog, child, family, or friends.

Reflections OF MY *Inner Garden*

Bhakti yoga is the yoga of the heart and the yoga of devotion. The gardens of Gaals' Little Acre were definitely bhakti gardens, for they were inspired, created, and maintained out of love and devotion—not only by me, but by all the gardeners I have been blessed to have over the years.

Most of the time when I am in my garden, I am in my soul. And in the center of my soul is my love of spirit—of God and guru. I am totally in the moment. And being in the moment, I am quiet, at peace, and in the flow of love. When I look into the face of a beautiful rose, and inhale its heady fragrance, it is like looking into the face of The Beloved.

I was surprised to discover that even the act of planning a new garden space is an opportunity for spiritual lessons. An important part of the design process is having the courage to follow your heart and to trust your intuition. Even though you may not have all the elements of your design in mind, if you trust—have faith—that it will all come together, it will. And experiencing it unfold and take form is exciting!

Create a garden that will be your sanctuary—a place of beauty where you can sit quietly, reflect, center, and bring peace into your life. Perhaps this is a space in which to meditate or pray, a space to celebrate the joys of life and to seek solace in times of sorrow. Or maybe a spot to sit, rest, and enjoy a cup of tea—allowing you to return to your day refreshed. Make this space meaningful and beautiful in your own eyes. The love you put into it will give it soul. And that feeling will resonate with other souls. Connecting to this inner garden is what transforms gardening into sadhana or devotional spiritual practice. Explore the gardens in the pages to come and see if they can give you some inspiration as you build your own special space.

Becky's Garden. When she was a baby, I planted her this child-size garden, so she, too, would get to experience the joys of gardening.

SPIRITUAL STATUES

- **HANUMAN:** the Hindu monkey god who represents bhakti yoga (love and devotion) and karma yoga (service to God)
- **QUAN YIN:** the Chinese goddess of compassion
- **SAINT FIACRE:** the patron saint of gardening
- **GANESH**: the Hindu elephant god of wisdom, remover of obstacles, and the god of new beginnings
- **THE VIRGIN MARY**
- **JESUS**
- **OUR LADY OF GUADALUPE**
- **SAINT FRANCIS OF ASSISI**: the patron saint of animals
- **DREAMCATCHER** (originated with the Ojibwe people)

The Spiritual Rose Garden · Soulful Sanctuaries ·

The Spiritual Rose Garden was my first garden with a spiritual theme. It felt like a natural expression of my love of God. One thing that drew me to spiritual practices that are primarily Hindu is that Hinduism, in its pure form, honors all religions, forms of God, spiritual paths, saints, and holy beings of all faiths—recognizing that there are many paths that lead to The One. With this garden, my intention was to represent and honor all major religions and the qualities they inspire and evoke, with statues, symbols, and roses.

At the entrance was a wide, wrought-iron arbor. This was made to support 'Compassion,' a beautiful, fragrant, pink-yellow-blend climbing Hybrid Tea rose. Once you entered through the arbor of 'Compassion,' there was a rustic little seating area with a bentwood love seat that faced the garden. All the roses here had names that went with the theme of the garden. Unlike my usual process when designing a garden, color combinations were not a consideration here. Rather, the names took priority, and they were all quite fragrant as well. The roses 'Angel Face,' 'Beloved,' 'Our Lady of Guadalupe,' 'Grace,' 'Love,' and 'Heaven on Earth' were just some of the roses I included here.

LEFT: 'Fortune's Double Yellow' (China, 1845). RIGHT: Roses from left to right: pink 'Our Lady of Guadalupe'; deep red 'Beloved'; the next red 'Maharaj-ji'; pink 'Sweet Surrender'; and finally, red 'Karma.'

SIGNS

- ❀ A bronze sign that read:

  It is God
  who made the garden
  grow in your hearts.
  —Corinthians 3:6

- ❀ A wooden Sufi winged heart
- ❀ The Star of David, with the word *Shalom*
- ❀ Three engraved rocks:
  - ❖ Peace
  - ❖ Remember
  - ❖ Namaste

MORE ROSE HIGHLIGHTS

'Sweet Surrender' (Hybrid Tea, 1983) This was planted at the far end of the garden and in front of a three-sided wrought-iron outline of a cathedral window.

'Maharaj-ji' This was originally a test rose for Jackson and Perkins that was never released, probably because the huge, fragrant roses are so heavy they cause the canes to hang down—but it is still a beautiful rose I named for my grandfather guru.

'Blessings' (Hybrid Tea, 1967) I imported these peach-colored roses from England long before they were available here in the U.S.

'Rosa Sancta' a.k.a. 'The Holy Rose' a.k.a. 'Rosa Richardii' (Damask, 1862) A mummified specimen of this rose was found in an Egyptian tomb dated AD 170. It is a lovely light-pink single, which, being a Damask rose, blooms only in the spring. It's about 2 feet high with supple canes cascading about 6 feet long. It would make a good ground cover.

'Peace' (Hybrid Tea, 1945) Known as "The World's Favorite Rose," 'Peace' is a joyful yet delicate pink-yellow-blend rose. It was introduced to mark the end of World War II.

RIGHT: Quan Yin statue with 'Sweet Inspiration' (Floribunda, after 1970). OPPOSITE PAGE: On the left side is 'Awakening' (Climber, 1990). On the right side is 'Compassion®' (Cl. Hybrid Tea, 1973).

Being the perfect embodiment of service and devotion, Hanuman is my *ishta-dev*—the form of God I am most drawn to. This was not a conscious decision. I did not think or feel, *Oh, what a cute little monkey. I think I'll fall in love with him.* It just happened.

So, about a year after moving to Gaals' Little Acre, I focused on a section where two clumps of banana trees were growing. I thought, *Gee, Hanuman would like it here—lots of bananas.* And I decided to create a garden in honor of Hanuman.

Almost everything in the garden is symbolic and purposeful, designed to honor, represent, and delight Hanuman. The color scheme is predominately red and yellow, which are Hanuman's colors. Depending on the season, there were gerbera daisies, monkey flowers (how perfect!), pansies, marigolds, tulips, English primrose, and red and yellow roses. Perhaps my favorite rose in this garden was the red-and-yellow 'Perfect Moment'—and there have been an abundance of those precious moments.

When my daughter was about six years old, I took her to a topiary class. Topiary is the art form of making animal or geometric shapes out of shrubs to decorate a garden. It is a lot of fun, very creative, and adds a wonderful touch of whimsy to any garden. The company that was hosting this workshop also created topiaries for Disneyland. We were given a choice of animal forms to create and decided to make mother and baby bunnies. For several hours, we stuffed and packed green-dyed sphagnum moss into the wire forms, wired them shut, and added eyes. They were darling. While making my bunny topiary, I got the brilliant idea of having a topiary made of Hanuman.

I'll never forget the moment I saw "my Hanuman." He was the standing form of Hanuman carrying a mountain of healing herbs. He was three feet tall and standing on a butcher block. I gasped and grinned from ear to ear. It was like this much-adored being that I had read so much about had come to life. Not only was he standing in front of me, but I was going to take him home. He would be available to me to receive his *darshan* (a meeting with a spiritual holy being). All I would have to do was visit him in my garden.

In addition to Hanuman, there were two other topiaries: a big heart and another pose of Hanuman, both pruned from eugenia shrubs. The second Hanuman was about eight feet tall and kneeled with one hand raised in blessing. In his other hand, he held a mala. When the wind blew, his blessing hand would sway gently, giving him the appearance of being alive. It took many years for this Hanuman to grow so he could be pruned into the desired form.

Om

The 60's Peace Garden

· Soulful Sanctuaries ·

In the early years of Gaals' Little Acre, we had two pygmy goats, Buffy and Toto. They taught us much about being playful. After they passed, the memory of their playfulness inspired me to create the "'60s Peace Garden." It was a creative challenge turning a fenced-in animal space into a garden, but I got brave and removed the fences, stripped away the boundaries, and began to play. It became one of my favorite places to eat breakfast and also became home to many hummingbirds.

In the center of this garden, I included a puja (prayer) table from a temple in India. It was an old, weathered stone table with the character that comes with aging. Planted behind the puja table was a 'Forest Pansy' redbud tree—a beautiful specimen with purple, heart-shaped leaves. It is deciduous, and in the spring, its branches are lined with tiny lavender-pink flowers.

Then there was the "psychedelic bed" with brightly colored flowers, ceramic magic mushrooms, and a plant that looks like marijuana, but is actually an aralia. There is a bright red miniature rose named 'High Spirits' and a rock engraved with "Beauty Is Everywhere." For sentimental reasons, I kept the goat house in the corner of this bed.

One of my favorite parts of this entire acre of gardens was a fence that spelled out "Be Here Now." The next section I created was a big peace symbol outlined in rocks and planted with Santa Barbara daisies. Walking around the pathway, we come to the bed I called the "Garden of Innocence" because the '60s were, among other things, a time of innocence. Some of the roses I included were 'Awakening,' and 'First Kiss,' and there was a 'Becky' shasta daisy.

Peter also built me a box on legs to hold three collages I made for this garden—one political, one spiritual, and the last, rock 'n' roll. One day, with friends, we played '60s music and painted the brick wall along the side of the garden with sayings and pictures from the decade.

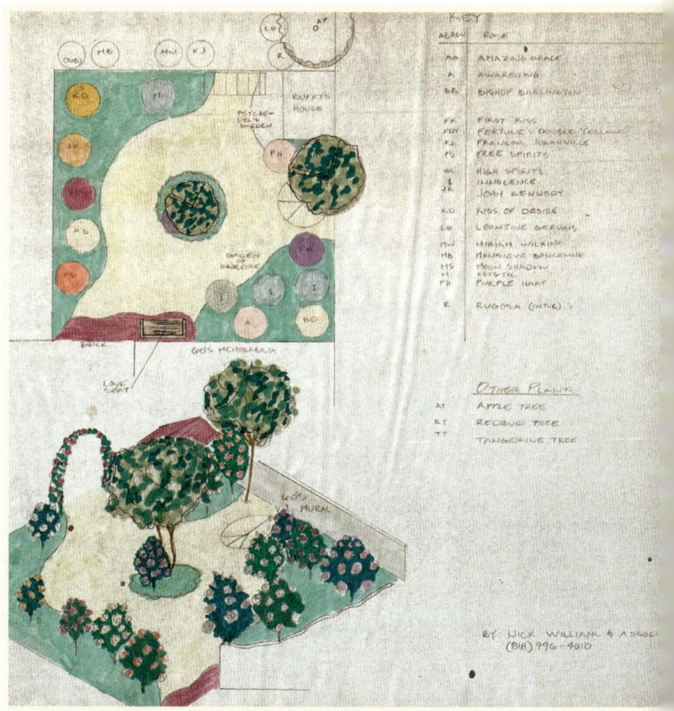

'60S PEACE GARDEN ROSES

- ❀ **'Awakening'** (Climber, 1990) *silvery pink.*
- ❀ **'Innocence'** (Miniature, 1997) *ivory.*
- ❀ **'Mystic'** (Shrub, 1994) *pink*
- ❀ **'Kiss of Desire'** (Climber, 1986) *white petals with hot pink edges; representing the sexual revolution of the '60s.*
- ❀ **'Purple Heart'** (Floribunda, 1999) *wine-red; representing the Vietnam War.*
- ❀ **'Summer of Love'** (Hybrid Tea, 2009) *white with coral-pink edges.*
- ❀ **'California Dreamin,™'** (Hybrid Tea, 2007) *mauve*
- ❀ **'Scarborough Fair'** (English, 2003) *light pink.*
- ❀ **'Mellow Yellow'** (Hybrid Tea, 2002) *yellow.*
- ❀ **'Woodstock'** (Miniature, 1999) *yellow-orange blend.*
- ❀ **'Amazing Grace'** (Hybrid Tea, 1973) *pink.*
- ❀ **'Love & Peace™'** (Hybrid Tea, 2002) *yellow with pink edges.*
- ❀ **'Baby Bloomer™'** (Miniature, 2007) *medium pink.*

LEFT: I thought it was important that Becky and I attend a local peace rally, so we made our signs and took this photo before we left. It's rather coincidental that I created the '60s Peace Garden on this very spot. ABOVE: Buffy and Toto. OPPOSITE: We kept the goathouse even after the goats were no longer with us. We built the garden around it with heliotrope in the foreground, shown here.

The Garden of the Joyful Heart

Soulful Sanctuaries

Have you ever lived with ducks? They are cute and fun and lay huge eggs, but boy, are they messy! During our years at Gaals' Little Acre, especially when Becky was young, we had ducks as part of our menagerie. When they were no longer with us, I was again gifted a new space. Since California law requires having an enclosure surrounding a pool or pond, I was forced to create another garden.

A beautiful wooden moon gate spurred the inspiration for this space. I originally named it "The Garden of Surrender," because from my understanding, the Eastern concept of surrender is one of the paths to peace of mind and connection to The One. Surrender involves living in the present moment, being open, having faith, and trusting life to unfold as it is meant to be. It is about letting go of thinking you are in control and surrendering to a higher power, which is not always easy.

One day Peter and I were walking through the garden. It was unusual for Peter to participate in garden design or details, but he made a suggestion. He said that the concept of "surrender" is one that is foreign to Western consciousness. He suggested renaming it "The Garden of the Joyful Heart," and so we did.

Looking through the moon gate, you could see the tall statue of Quan Yin, the Chinese goddess of compassion. And seated on the edge of the pond was a statue of Buddha. A covered, carved Indian bench beckoned you to sit in the shade, meditate, and listen to the fountain trickling into the pond. At the entrance there was a large gong with which you could announce your arrival and departure.

Peter planted a California pepper tree shortly after we moved to Santa Paula. It was huge and had a gnarled, beautiful trunk that gave it the appearance of an ancient tree. Its gentle, weeping branches became the canopy of this garden. Some of those branches form what I interpret as the "veils of illusion" from William James's theories of consciousness. So, you can actually look through these "filmiest of screens" and imagine a different reality beyond. This provides inspiration to trust and surrender to the Divine source of all, merging with the beauty of the Universe.

A special part of this garden was a small altar to Ganesh. I put out a wooden bowl with an assortment of rocks and a waterproof pen and encouraged visitors to invest their rock with whatever they would like to surrender and offer it to Ganesh, and he could help them. These are usually things we know about ourselves that keep us from being the beautiful souls that we truly are, that keep us from being happy, content, and at peace. People have written things like "fear," "anger," "control," "greed," and "self-pity." My favorite, though, was "the sorrow of partings."

I also included the tiny red-leaf 'Threadleaf' Japanese maple, one of my favorite trees. Their soft, graceful, and flexible branches and foliage are so lovely, as is their muted maroon color. While appearing quite fragile, they are surprisingly resilient. They survive heavy rainstorms and Santa Ana winds, and

'Ambridge Rose' (English shrub, 1986) is in the foreground, and the one behind it (same color) is 'Marie Curie®' (Floribunda, 1997).

at the end of their season, most of the dead leaves continue to hang on tenaciously. Part of the late winter or early spring garden work involves removing these dead leaves. Because of the delicacy involved, much of the pruning of Japanese maples is best done with bare fingers, which also allows an intimate connection with the tree. The new leaves are beginning to open or have recently leafed out. Removing the dead leaves makes space for the new leaves. Just as the Japanese maples need a little help in letting go, at times we all need a little help in letting go of what is keeping us from living from our souls—living from the space of love—and letting go into the next moment.

BELOW: 'The Wedgewood Rose' (Cl. English, 2009). RIGHT: Inside the Garden of the Joyful Heart, looking through the moon gate toward the front door of the house. OPPOSITE TOP: Ganesh. OPPOSITE MIDDLE: The original duck pond. OPPOSITE BOTTOM: Our Puli, Rami, liked to visit Daisy and Donald—the ducks who lived at the pond before we transformed it into a garden.

DUCKS'
VILLAGE

The Japanese Garden

· Soulful Sanctuaries ·

I have always loved Japanese gardens. Perhaps it is the simplicity, the attention to detail, the orderliness, and the beauty of the plants usually seen in a Japanese garden. I think it is all of that along with the traditions and philosophy represented. But most of all it is the feelings that are evoked—those of serenity, sacredness, order, tranquility—a sense of place and peace. When I would work in this garden, it required a great deal of precise detail work. My mind would be quiet. As I listened the sounds of the fountain, breeze, and birds and focused my attention on the plants, I was totally present.

ABOVE: The beginning of the Japanese Garden.

After we remodeled our house, we had a small space between the two main parts of the house that was visible from the kitchen and the primary bedroom. It proved to be the perfect space for my little Japanese garden.

We had already built the house around our wisteria. It was well worth it, as the wisteria soon covered the inner outline of that garden, giving us an exceptional springtime gift of showering racemes of the beautiful lavender flowers and a sense of grace.

As beautiful as the wisteria was, the star of this garden was my bodhi tree, *Ficus religiosa*. This is truly a sacred tree. In the fourth century, young prince Siddhartha Gautama, who had led a very sheltered life, broke away from the castle where he was raised to see beyond what he sensed was only a protected part of the world. Once exposed to humanity, he saw all the suffering that existed in the world and wanted to be free of that. So he traveled and studied with Hindu saints and teachers in search of enlightenment. After many years, it was while meditating under the bodhi tree that Siddhartha attained enlightenment and became the Buddha, which means "The Enlightened One." This site, located in Northern India in Bodh Gaya in the state of Bihar, is a cherished site of pilgrimage for Buddhists and spiritual seekers. The bodhi tree, with its graceful leaves that have a pointed tip, has become a symbol of spirituality.

So, knowing this history, you can imagine my delight when my garden guru presented me with a bodhi tree in a one-gallon container. That little tree moved with us to Santa Paula, and it didn't

take it long to grow up. It thrived in my Japanese garden, at about 50 feet tall. It is rare to see a bodhi tree in Southern California. In fact, I have never seen another one.

Creating Gardens FOR THE *Inner Child*

In the garden of the inner child, which exists in adults as well as children, it is always springtime. It is a happy place—a feeling of innocence, wonder, joy, and delight. There is a magical belief that anything is possible. The inner child loves to play and have fun. And all our life experiences combine and influence who we eventually become. Do you remember making mud pies? Or splashing around in the water from a garden hose, sprinklers, or in a wading pool?

Planting a seed in the garden is an exercise in faith. You don't know if it will come up or if it will produce. In life, every act is a seed, and you have no idea how it will bear fruit or might possibly change the life of somebody.

I found this to be true when gardening with children. If children are involved in gardening at a young age, on one level or another, it will be a connection to that precious inner child that will return to them in a meaningful way throughout their lives. Harvesting the fruits of your experience and sharing them with children is fun and helps us keep in touch with our own inner child and that sense of wonder.

When my Becky was in preschool, we had her whole class over to share in the wonders of the garden. I remember those sweet, innocent little faces in awe of seeing how food grows. In our agricultural area, all children had seen orchards of oranges, avocados, and lemons, and fields of strawberries—but they had not necessarily seen peas growing in the garden, nor gotten to squeeze them from their shells and eat them—right there—where they grew. Apples, peaches, and pears hanging from the trees, tomatoes and cucumbers dangling from their vines—all were delightful surprises to the children. And then there was the smelling of everything—roses, sweet peas, gardenias, orange blossoms, jasmine, lilac, lavender—just a feast for the senses. Many of my favorite gardens were themed especially for children or the young at heart.

LEFT: Becky working in her garden.
RIGHT: The wishing well Peter built for the Fairy Tale Garden.

Believe

Opening the small wooden gate of my Secret Garden and closing it behind me gave me a feeling of retreating from the world. Just beyond the gate there was an arbor covered with 'Cl. Maman Cochet'—a pink climbing tea rose.

At the beginning of autumn, my garden would be wonderfully overgrown. Entering the garden under the arbor covered with the lovely pink roses of 'Cl. Maman Cochet,' the Alsroemeria (Peruvian Lily) spilled onto the entryway. I was always reminded of the classic book *The Secret Garden* by Frances Hodgson Burnett. As if by magic, I felt like Mary, the little girl in the book who has discovered an old, neglected, overgrown garden—surrounded by walls—and decides to tame and restore it.

My garden was not neglected, but for approximately half of each year, I enjoyed being that little girl nurturing that Secret Garden. Unlike its namesake, though, my garden was not enclosed by high walls made of old rock. Instead, my Secret Garden had living walls made of roses—ramblers, climbers, musk roses, fragrant English Roses, and French Guillot roses. When sitting under one of the arbors, maybe with a cup of tea, I was completely hidden and surrounded by roses, herbs, and a few topiaries. I always felt a great sense of peace.

To know a garden intimately is one of life's greatest pleasures. For a seriously devoted gardener, there is an unspoken commitment that the gardener will give attention to the garden in all its phases—infancy, full bloom, and as it ages. The gardener assumes the responsibility of learning how to provide the best life for the garden: to observe the daily changes, in sickness and in health; to help it achieve its full potential; to love and care for the garden through all the seasons of its life. The garden is a teacher and can deepen the gardener's appreciation of the changing phases of life. Mary expresses it best when she says, "If you look the right way, you can see the whole world is a garden."

LEFT: The rose over the arbor entrance is a pink 'Cl. Maman Cochet' (Cl. Tea, 1906). TOP: Evolving Secret Garden. ABOVE MIDDLE: One end of the Secret Garden, years after being established. The rose 'Cecile Brunner' (Cl. Polyantha, 1881) covered the rabbit run and the shaded home of *Cymbidium* orchids.

The Fairy Tale Garden

· Soulful Sanctuaries ·

On one of my frequent trips to the nursery, I found myself standing face-to-face with a statue of Peter Rabbit. He was my spontaneous inspiration for this garden. Imagine my delight when, in a different area of the nursery, I spotted statues of Alice in Wonderland, the White Rabbit, and the Mad Hatter! I was so excited! My family was surprised (but, knowing me, not too surprised) when I brought these "friends" home.

And one day, driving down the main street through Summerland, just south of Santa Barbara, I spotted an adorable little gazebo. Instantly picturing tea parties in the gazebo, I slammed on the brakes, turned around, and brought it home.

I wasn't quite sure where this garden would be located, but I knew I would find just the right space. I often feel, though, like I am a garden looking for a place to manifest.

Thanks to the help of my devoted gardeners, we found the right spot and the garden materialized easily. We planted two climbing roses, the yellow-and-ruby-red 'Dreams Come True™' and the pastel-pink 'Flower Girl,' to adorn the gazebo, adding a touch of magic to this fantasy garden. We also added a fuchsia tree (because the flowers look like little ballerinas), pansies, and 'Johnny Jump Up' violas.

From then on, Becky and I were on the lookout for other beings to add to this theme garden. Over the years, we were joined by Bambi and Thumper; Mickey, Minnie, and Donald; Mr. Toad; a few large metal butterflies and ladybugs; Winnie the Pooh; Peter Pan (who unusually had glass wings); and a fairy family.

Peter had four children when we married, so I was blessed with several grandchildren, even when my Becky was still young. When they all visited, we often added a few touches to this garden—like a fairy house with seed pods collected for furniture. Peter also built me a wishing well, and visiting children threw in pennies and made their wishes. A fun time was had by all.

TALE GARDEN

OPPOSITE: "Dumbo" topiary.
LEFT, TOP: A hummingbird nest in Peter's magnolia tree. LEFT, BOTTOM: 'Flower Girl' (Climber, 1998). This climbing rose grew over the entrance to our Fairy Tale Garden gazebo.
BELOW: Peter Pan.

Peter's Train Garden

Soulful Sanctuaries

Knowing of Peter's childhood fascination with trains, one Christmas I bought him a train "starter kit"—an engine, several cars, and enough track to go around our Christmas tree. He was unbelievably delighted and immediately started putting the track together. In no time at all, there was a train circling our Christmas tree.

Little did I know what a sensitive inner child I had touched! As soon as the children and grandchildren left after the holidays, my dear husband pushed all the furniture in our family room to one end, brought in wood and tools, and started to build a three-foot-high layout for what turned out to be "Peter's Train Garden."

Fortunately, he built the layout in sections so it could eventually be relocated onto the driveway in front of his garage. The project gave him so much pleasure, and a fabulous train garden it was! It was about 20 feet by 10 feet—a charming miniature world.

The wooden layout was surrounded by concrete blocks and good soil with appropriate drainage so we could landscape. It could accommodate three trains simultaneously—one of them was a steam locomotive that Peter especially loved. He built trestles and bridges and villages. He ordered a kit designed by an architect that came with blueprints and 10,000 little pieces of wood. With these, he built a train station and hotel (I made the lace curtains) and a cute general store. My part was landscaping this miniature world with live plants. In a unique, beautiful acre of gardens, it was Peter's Train Garden that stole everyone's heart!

OPPOSITE: I built this little Victorian house for one end of the Train Garden. BELOW: Peter built this train station and inn out of many, many tiny pieces of wood.

731

"Bread feeds the body, indeed,
but flowers feed also the soul."

—THE QURAN

BRINGING IT HOME

Garden Practice

CREATE A SACRED GARDEN OR ALTAR IN YOUR GARDEN

I invite you to express love—your love of nature, garden, or spirit in whatever way feels right for you. Translate a spiritual garden theme as an expression of your unique inner garden. It can be as simple as a comfortable chair beneath a tree. A space to rest, to *be* in the presence of nature—a space for remembrance. Or you can create a garden with a spiritual theme, similar to my Spiritual Rose Garden.

Make this a sanctuary–a holy space, set apart from the world.

Actually, that is what a garden that has soul is.

PASS IT ON

Sharing your passion for your garden and love of nature is a gift. Especially to your children or friends, who will pass it on to their children and friends.

Becky once called me and said, "Mom, I'm turning into you!" Surprised to hear this, I asked her what she meant. She told me she had just been to the nursery and bought herbs and marigolds and was going to plant an herb garden. I absolutely loved that!

For this practice, take the time to create a garden with a child or local kindergarten class. You may just be giving those children a lifetime relationship with gardening.

OPPOSITE: The rose 'Beloved' grew right into Buddha's lap.
RIGHT: 'Ingrid Bergman®' (Hybrid Tea, 1984).

BRINGING IT HOME

Spiritual Practice

BECOMING LOVING AWARENESS

A wonderful way of relating from your soul, rather than from your ego and mind, is Ram Dass's practice of "loving awareness."

In his later years, one of Ram Dass's primary teachings was that of becoming loving awareness. Having evolved into a being who manifested love, he was the perfect one to show us how to get there. He taught that to change levels of consciousness from the worldly ego mind-centered level to your spiritual level or—in other words—to bring your awareness from your head into your heart, from your ego into your soul, repeat to yourself, "I am loving awareness, I am loving awareness, I am loving awareness . . ."

After a short while, just repeat "loving awareness," until you remember who you really are and arrive at that precious heart space. You can use "I am loving awareness" as a mantra.

GARDENING AS SADHANA

Sadhana is an ego-transcending spiritual practice that leads to the intended goal of realization of the Divine. More simply expressed, sadhana is one's spiritual path. I see gardening as a devotional practice. My heart opens as I care for each rose or plant, deciding exactly where to prune or deadhead for optimum growth, and nurturing the garden so that it will reach its full potential as a manifestation of the Divine.

The garden is the perfect place for doing spiritual practices: cutting and offering flowers to deities with devotion; practicing *parikrama* (circumambulating); saying prayers; meditating; practicing tai chi and yoga; connecting with the peace, beauty, and changes of nature; and experiencing reminders of grace.

Our happiness is built by intention and attitude. Look every day for love, beauty, humor, and tenderness. Look for the feeling of grace. It is all around us. Expect to find it. Remember.

> *"Being Love is a supreme transformative act."*
>
> —RAM DASS

OPPOSITE: Spirit house occupied by the goddess Lakshmi.

From The Garden To The Kitchen

Flowerpot CUPCAKES

This is one of the cutest, easiest desserts ever! In fact, these cupcakes are so cute, people don't want to eat them. This is also a fun project to make with a child (not to mention your own inner child). Collect a few key parts before assembling.

GATHER YOUR SUPPLIES:

- CLAY POTS AND SAUCERS. Buy 2-inch-diameter clay pots and their saucers for as many cupcakes as you intend to serve. Reserve these pots only for baking.
- CHOCOLATE ROCKS. Yes, chocolate rocks exist. They are small candies that look like pebbles. I find these at Somis Nut House in Somis, California, which is near me. But they are also available at specialty candy stores and online. They are an important feature of this adorable dessert.
- ORGANIC ROSEBUDS. From your garden, pick organically grown rosebuds, one for each cupcake you plan to serve.
- FRESH PARSLEY. You'll need a few sprigs.
- CRUMBLED OREO COOKIES. You can buy these already crushed or take each whole cookie apart like you did when you were a kid and scrape away the filling. Put the cookies in a zip-top plastic bag and crush them. What you do with the leftover cookie filling can be your secret.
- CUPCAKE RECIPE. For the cupcake itself, you can bake your own favorite recipe and frost them, or if you don't have the time or inclination to make them yourself, buy carrot cake cupcakes from Trader Joe's (they are already frosted and taste yummy).

Now for the creative part:

1. Place each flowerpot inside a saucer.
2. Set each frosted cupcake in its paper baking cup into the flowerpot.
3. Cover the frosting of the cupcake with the crushed Oreo cookies. This will be your "dirt."
4. "Plant" a rosebud in the center of each cupcake. The rosebud pictured here is 'Cl. Cecile Brunner.'
5. Add small pieces of parsley around the rosebud as its "leaves."
6. Arrange the chocolate rocks around the saucer. Be sure and tell your guests that the rocks are edible.
7. These cupcakes are so cute you can't help but smile. And take a picture.

There is a Season

CHAPTER FIVE

Observing the ebb and flow of the seasons in the garden, we learn about the fleeting nature of beauty as well as life's inevitable transitions. The seasons give structure to life. Nature presents us with cyclical changes of birth, growth, and death. They all contribute to the rhythm and rituals of our lives. The seasons flow one into another, one season giving way to the next. Each season feels different. There is a change in weather and temperature, the light is different, we dress differently, eat differently, plant differently, have different activities. Each season is associated with symbols, fragrances, food, flowers, how we decorate our homes, and celebrations with family and friends. In all seasons, the garden facilitates our connection to time.

"It was the best of times; it was the worst of times . . .
it was the season of Light, it was the season of Darkness,
it was the spring of hope; it was the winter of despair."

—CHARLES DICKENS, *A Tale of Two Cities*

Transitions

And so it is with the seasons of our lives. The inner garden, the seasons can interpenetrate each other. There is always an opportunity for springtime in our spirit, based on our spiritual awareness. There is always the opportunity for new life, ideas, new ways of perceiving, fresh new forms of beauty, and—always—love.

Summer is time for play and a change in our usual routines, as well as for appreciating our work that yields beauty and abundance. Autumn is a time to harvest the fruits of our efforts. And winter brings dormancy—of plants and ideas alike—the sorrows of parting that arise daily in ways that are little or devastating, and, each night, a time for rest. In the garden of our souls, it is all possible, all the time.

"To everything there is a season, and a time to every purpose under the heaven."

—ECCLESIASTES 3:1

SPRING

THE *Passions* AND *Wonder* OF *Life*

The spring garden is a feast for the senses. The primary feeling that spring evokes is one of love—an expansive love for everything and everyone—and grateful for being alive and experiencing the grace of Mother Nature. Is it any wonder that spring is my favorite season?

The transition to spring is a welcome one. As the sleeping garden begins to awaken, the first signs of spring are numerous and evident. Walking along the garden path, I was always delighted to see and sense new life and the freshness and tenderness of youth. There is a palette of spring colors—pastels accented with bursts of brightness. Birds return to sing, often accompanied by the sweet chirping of their babies in nests throughout the garden. And the hummingbirds dart here and there with their delightful energy.

With the return of longer periods of daylight warming the earth, our spirits are lifted. It is a time of rebirth and resilience, and we often feel an increase in energy and vitality. We begin eating and dressing lighter. Some of this energy is traditionally directed toward "spring cleaning" both in the home and in both the outer and inner gardens. In the outer garden, this includes completing the winter cleanup in early spring— cultivating and amending the soil (especially for the roses), adding fertilizer, applying compost as mulch, and spraying dormant oil before the roses leaf out, revealing their first young, beautiful leaves of the year. And in the inner garden, we cultivate love.

Annuals and bulbs planted in the fall begin to bloom now. My favorites are pansies, violas, snapdragons, stock, sweet peas, ranunculus, tulips, daffodils, narcissus, columbine, heuchera, iris, foxglove, Canterbury bells, delphiniums, larkspur, lupine, and nemesia. Also emerging are racemes of cascading wisteria, magnificent magnolias, lilac, Chinese tree peonies, sweet peach and apple blossoms, and fragrant jasmine and orange blossoms. And last, but certainly not least, the roses are now fully leafing out and beginning to bloom.

For a period of two to four weeks, the garden is a picture of absolute perfection, and very little deadheading is needed. Embracing springtime, it is possible to feel the Divine manifested everywhere in everything.

LEFT: 'Lady Banks' Rose', a.k.a. the rose that ate the roof! That was just our nickname for it, but it did actually crack our rain gutters. *Rosa banksiae* is the world's largest rose. That specimen lives and thrives in Tombstone, Arizona. It was planted in 1885, covers over 8,000 square feet, and the circumference of the trunk is 12 feet!

"The spring came suddenly, bursting upon the world as a child bursts into a room, with a laugh and a shout and hands full of flowers."

—HENRY WADSWORTH LONGFELLOW

AWAKENING THE INNER GARDEN IN SPRING

In the inner garden, there is a sense of hope and possibility and dreams fulfilled in springtime. Spring fever is truly a matter of the heart—and when you feel it, it is all so beautifully apparent. There is a yearning to be outside with nature. There is a restlessness in your soul and perhaps an urge to make changes or take on new creative projects. There is a sense of wonder at the incredible beauty that reminds us of the spiritual nature of being alive.

Spring fever is a form of resting in the state of love. We embrace nature, and nature embraces us.

"I've always thought my flowers had souls."

—MYRTLE REED, *Lavender and Old Lace*

Sandy's
LEMON TEA CAKE

Always a big favorite! This recipe makes great use of the lemon thyme in your garden and always reminds me of springtime.

FOR THE CAKE

2 cups all-purpose flour

2 teaspoons baking powder

¼ teaspoon salt

6 tablespoons butter, softened

1 cup sugar

2 eggs

1 tablespoon grated lemon zest

2 tablespoons fresh lemon juice

2 tablespoons fresh lemon thyme leaves, from your garden

⅔ cup milk

FOR THE GLAZE

2 tablespoons fresh lemon juice

½ cup sifted powdered sugar

MAKES 1 (9-BY-5-INCH) LOAF

To make the cake

1. Preheat the oven to 325°F. Grease and flour a 9-by-5-inch loaf pan.
2. In a medium bowl, mix together the flour, baking powder, and salt. Set aside.
3. In a stand mixer, beat the butter and gradually add the sugar, beating until fluffy, about 2 minutes.
4. Add the eggs, one at a time, beating well after each addition. Add the lemon zest, lemon juice, and lemon thyme and beat until well mixed.
5. Add the flour mixture alternately with the milk, beating on low until well mixed. Pour the batter into the loaf pan.
6. Bake for 55 to 60 minutes, or until the top is golden and a toothpick inserted into the center comes out clean. Let cool in the pan on a wire rack for 10 minutes. Remove the cake from the pan and let cool completely.

To make the glaze and serve

1. In a medium bowl, mix together the lemon juice with powdered sugar until smooth and pourable.
2. Drizzle the glaze over the top of the cake. Cut into slices and serve.

SUMMER

Peaches AND *Beaches*

Summer, like all the seasons, is a state of mind. It is giving ourselves permission to relax and enjoy life. In the process, we may find that dreams can become more real. The days grow longer, and the extra light allows for more gardening and pleasant evening activities. The days grow warmer, encouraging us to shed layers of clothes, be more playful, go barefoot, go to the beach, and have picnics. We often have more leisure time to play or work on projects, alone or with family or friends.

The summer garden, blossoming into fullness, continues to manifest the beauty and growth initiated in spring. There is an abundance of brighter colors in the garden and energy moves up from the earth like flowers dancing.

For me, the fragrance of summer is that of roses and salty sea air—though not necessarily simultaneously. Roses continue to bloom, as well as hydrangeas, sunflowers, dahlias, lavender, marigolds, cosmos, petunias, nemesia, lobelia, and impatiens—to name a few. *Ceratostigma*, the beautiful ground cover in my woodland garden that leafed out in spring with bronze-colored leaves, now begins to bloom with its blue flowers. This is the ground cover form of the plumbago bush. In the fall, it loses its leaves. This allows the planted bulbs to emerge in early spring before that cycle repeats itself.

As always, the cycle of gardening continues—as soon as the sweet peas finish in late spring/early summer, we collect their seeds. In the space where the sweet peas grew, it is time to plant corn and Indian corn and the pumpkin patch.

"If we could see the miracle of a single flower clearly, our whole life would change."

—JACK KORNFIELD

SUMMER'S HARVEST

I know it is summer when I must eat our nectarines outside because they are so juicy. The summer brings a bounty of peaches and nectarines, melons, grapes, citrus, as well as never-ending amounts of summer squash, eggplants, peppers, cucumbers, avocados, tomatoes, and beans.

The star of the harvest for our garden was Peter's blackberries. They began in May and finished in mid-July. Everyone delighted in picking berries and eating them fresh off the vine—even the doggies, who claimed the bottom branches as their own. Of course we could do that because they were organic! The yield of these vines was amazing, and we harvested berries by the bucketful. The next step in processing the berries was washing them and flash freezing them. That way, they could be used in jam or stored for later use. We would save some of the fresh berries for fruit salads, smoothies, and occasional toppings for ice cream.

Then there was canning Peter's delicious blackberry jam. Yum, yum, yum! For some reason, we inevitably started canning Memorial Day weekend—just when the weather turned hot.

HOW TO PICK A RIPE MELON

Not many home gardeners attempt to grow their own melons, but eating them is part of summer.

CANTALOUPE: Select one that is light-colored and has a lot of webbing or netting on the outside. Turn the melon to the end opposite the blossom end and press with your thumbs. If gentle pressure makes the melon "give," it is ripe.

HONEYDEW: With one hand, slide your fingers along the outside of the melon. If it feels sticky, it is ripe.

WATERMELON: Thump it. You want to hear a hollow sound. Then it is ripe.

"And so with the sunshine and the great bursts of leaves growing on the trees, just as things grow fast in movies, I had that familiar conviction that life was beginning over again with the summer."

—F. SCOTT FITZGERALD, *The Great Gatsby*

AWAKENING THE INNER GARDEN IN SUMMER

In the soul, too, summer represents a time of growth and relaxation—easygoing, playful, and in touch with your own nature, as well as with Mother Nature.

And since we may have more leisure time during the summer, perhaps we can pay more attention to little things that are always important. For example, summer vacation from school gave us more time to be with our friends. It is said that friends are flowers in life's garden, and that is true. The beauty of a true friendship is to be there for each other through the joys and sorrows of life.

SUMMER CANNING

Since we were fortunate to have a Wolf range with six burners, fruit from our own trees, and family and friends who loved our preserves and pickles, when we canned, we did so in large batches. You can preserve your bounty in whatever quantities you like according to your supply of fruit and available time.

GENERAL CANNING INSTRUCTIONS

- A canner usually holds up to seven 32-ounce jars or nine 16-ounce jars.
- It is important that all jars, lids, and whatever you are canning are hot when putting the food into the jars.
- There must be a proper amount of headspace between the food and the top of the jar—I mention this in each recipe—and the tops of the jars must be wiped clean to allow for a complete seal.
- In a separate small pot, the ilid inserts need to be boiled for 10 minutes, then kept in the hot water until ready to use.
- When your product is cooked, hot, and ready to be canned, remove one or two jars at a time from the hot water bath. Using a funnel, ladle the product into the hot jar, wipe the edge of the jar with a clean, damp paper towel, remove the insert from the hot water and place on the jar, and tighten the lid. Using a jar lifter, place into the canner filled with hot water.
- The tops of the jars should be submerged in the boiling water. For 16-ounce jars or smaller, boil for 10 minutes. If using jars between 16 and 32 ounces, boil for 20 minutes. Each recipe has recommendations for the jar size recommended.
- When it is time to remove the jars from the canner, do so carefully with a jar

lifter, and place the hot jars on a towel.

❀ After cooling, check to make sure the jars are sealed by pressing your finger into the center of the lid. You should not feel or hear a *click*. A click would indicate that the jar is not sealed and that means the food is not preserved. If that happens, refrigerate the filled jars and use them within a few weeks.

FLASH FREEZING BERRIES

To freeze your berries, partially fill a clean sink with cold water. Line a cookie sheet with waxed paper. Gently dump all the berries into the water. Swish them around to remove any loose debris, leaves, and stems. Gently scoop up a handful of berries and spread them out on the cookie sheet in a single layer. Depending on how many berries you have, you may need to use more than one cookie sheet. Place the cookie sheet filled with berries in the freezer until the berries are frozen solid, at least eight hours or overnight. Remove the cookie sheet from the freezer and transfer the berries to zip-top plastic bags. Return the berries to the freezer. They can be frozen for up to 12 months.

If you plan to make jam the same day, wash the berries as instructed above. Place the berries in a large bowl and crush them with a potato masher. If you plan to can the next day, store the crushed berries in wide-mouth Mason jars in the refrigerator.

The original Mason jars were capable of holding hot food and were considered to be freezer safe, as well as for basic storage. Currently, there seems to be a variety of Mason jars that have different purposes. Many are decorative and intended for storage only at room temperature. So be sure to check your jars' intended use.

From The Garden • To The Kitchen •

Peter's AMAZING BLACKBERRY JAM

Just before making jam (or the night before if you are making large batches), it is necessary to prepare a pectin and calcium mixture, which helps jam to jell. Loquats are very perishable and will only last for about three days. If you don't have a loquat tree like we did, just use additional crushed blackberries.

FOR CANNING

Canner

6 (8-ounce) Mason jars with lids and rings

Small pot, for boiling lids and rings

FOR THE PECTIN MIXTURE

2 (8-ounce) Mason jars

1 tablespoon Pomona's Universal Pectin with calcium powder

½ cup sugar

FOR THE JAM

4 cups crushed blackberries, fresh or frozen and thawed

2 cups loquat puree or an additional 2 cups crushed blackberries

2½ cups sugar (if using only blackberries, use 3 cups sugar)

2 tablespoons fresh lemon juice

MAKES 6 (8-OUNCE) JARS

To prepare the canning jars

1. Follow the detailed General Canning Instructions on page 146.

To make the pectin mixture

1. In one Mason jar, combine the pectin and sugar. Cover and shake until well mixed. Set aside.
2. In the other Mason jar, combine 1 teaspoon calcium powder and 1 cup water. Cover and shake until well mixed. Set aside.

To make the jam.

1. In a large, heavy pot over medium-high heat, combine the blackberries, loquat puree, and sugar. Add the lemon juice and stir until combined.
2. Bring the mixture to a rolling boil, stirring occasionally. Slowly mix in the pectin mixture until well combined. Return to a boil and cook for 2 minutes. Remove from the heat.
3. Shake the Mason jar with the calcium mixture. Add 1 tablespoon of the calcium mixture to the fruit mixture and stir until well combined.
4. Remove the sterilized canning jars from the canner. Spoon the fruit mixture into the jars, leaving ¼-inch headspace. Wipe the rims of the jars clean with a paper towel or kitchen towel. Top with the lids and screw on the rings.
5. Return the sealed jars to the canner and bring the water to a boil over medium-high heat. Boil for 10 minutes.
6. Remove the jars from the canner and place them on kitchen towels. Listen for the *pop, pop, pop,* indicating your jars have properly sealed.
7. If you have enough fruit to double this recipe, make the jam in batches.

Notes:

Extra calcium mixture can be stored in a Mason jar in the refrigerator for a few months. Shake before using.

If the berries are frozen, you can take them out of the freezer the night before to defrost.

From The Garden To The Kitchen

LEMON CURD

I love lemon curd! It makes a great gift, so sometimes I triple this recipe, in which case it yields about seven 8-ounce jars.

FOR THE CANNING

Canner

2 (8-ounce) Mason jars with lids and rings

Small pot, for boiling lids and rings

FOR THE LEMON CURD

Zest of 3 large lemons

Juice of 2 large lemons

8 ounces sugar

4 ounces butter

2 eggs

MAKES 2 (8-OUNCE) JARS

To prepare the canning jars

1. Follow the detailed General Canning Instructions on page 146.

To make the lemon curd

1. In a double boiler, add enough water to the lower pan so it does not touch the upper pan.
2. Combine the lemon zest, lemon juice, sugar, and butter in the top pan and place the double boiler over medium heat. Cook, stirring from time to time, until the butter and sugar have melted.
3. Add the beaten eggs and continue cooking, stirring often, until the mixture coats the back of a wooden spoon.
4. Fill the sterilized jars with the lemon mixture, leaving ¼-inch headspace. Wipe the rims of the jar clean with a paper towel or kitchen towel. Top with the lids and screw on the rings.
5. Return the sealed jars to the canner and bring the water to a boil over medium-high heat. Boil for 10 minutes.
6. Remove the jars from the canner and place them on kitchen towels. Listen for the *pop, pop, pop*, indicating your jars have properly sealed.

AUTUMN

Harvesting THE *Fruits* AND *Aging*

Oh, how I love autumn! The transition from summer to fall is refreshing and most welcome. The intensity of the weather softens and cools. Bright summer colors fade out into the rich tones of pumpkins, corn, and turning leaves—shades of bronze, red, yellow, and maroon. In my Southern California garden, the stars of autumn color were the persimmons, pomegranates, bodhi tree, and, most of all, Boston ivy. At the entrance to the kitchen door, the Chinese pistache stood in the foreground of the ivy-covered house, which echoed the beautiful autumn colors of the pistache. A variety of deciduous trees completed the seasonal appearance.

The fall bloom of roses is magnificent! In autumn, many roses develop a deeper, richer intensity, while some become quite ethereal. You can clearly see the changes they are going through. Theoretically, this is the last bloom of roses of the year, although, in defiance, they often refuse to rest and continue to bloom until Christmas.

As autumn progresses, it becomes colder outside and cozier inside—a nesting time before winter arrives. We experience changes in the food we eat, enjoy many harvest festivals, prepare for the approaching holidays by decorating our homes, and gather with family and friends to celebrate holiday rituals.

In the garden, we witness the completion of the growth that started in the spring. The fall garden stars flowers like dahlias (like the large 'Dinnerplate' variety, as well as smaller forms in shades of purples, pinks, and yellow-orange-beige), zinnias, asters, and sunflowers. Alongside these blooms, we harvest the bounty of the garden, clean up thoroughly, and prepare for fall planting.

"And all the lives we ever lived and
all the lives to be are full of trees
and changing leaves . . ."
—VIRGINIA WOOLF, *To the Lighthouse*

THE ABUNDANT HARVEST

At Gaals' Little Acre, it seemed like it was always harvest time, but autumn provided an especially beautiful abundance. Our mudroom was crowded with baskets filled with nature's bounty. I loved to decorate my kitchen and the front of the house with pumpkins, corn stalks, and ornamental corn from the garden, often adding a bale of hay from the local feed store.

As I wandered through my fall garden, feeling the crisp, cool air, I would take note of what needed harvesting, processing, and sharing.

Apples: Harvest to make apple pie, apple cobbler, chunky cinnamon applesauce, Dutch apple cake, apple butter, and just apples for eating.

Pomegranates: Harvest for juice, to sprinkle in salads, and to dry for decoration.

Avocados: Continue harvesting, and use them with everything, including guacamole.

Valencia oranges: Continue harvesting. These are often the least attractive ones, now at the end of their season, but they are the sweetest oranges of the year, and they make the best orange juice.

Seckel pears: These are delicious dessert pears and a gourmet treat fresh or poached in a simple sugar syrup. They are also good for canning, and were a favorite treat of our Shih Tzu, Daisy.

Bartlett pears: Eat these fresh! They are also good for pear upside-down cake.

Fuyu (Japanese) persimmons: These are my favorite for eating from the branch (eaten like an apple). They are also the favorite of many of our friends, so they disappeared quickly. The best chutney I make is persimmon and dried apricot—see recipe on page 162.

Hachiya persimmons: These are just beginning to turn orange at the beginning of the fall. It won't be long before this beautiful, abundant crop allows me to bake persimmon bread (recipe on page 171), while the leaves of this huge, old tree provide us with a show of beautiful colors. They are larger than Fuyus and slightly oval. The pulp is eaten or used to bake with when it becomes soft. It is a very sensuous fruit. Make a note: If eaten before they are ripe, Hachiyas will make your mouth pucker.

Pumpkins and winter squash: Use for decorating and roasting. It's such fun for the child within each of us to grow our own pumpkin patch! We grew varieties from the little white 'Baby Boo' and 'Cinderella' pumpkins (one always went in front of the Fairy Tale Garden) to the huge 'Big Max.'

Ornamental corn: This is my daughter's and my sentimental favorite. Over the years, we spent many a happy hour husking and marveling at Mother Nature's artistry in creating the colors and patterns in such an awesome array. Each one was like opening a treasure. As we have gotten older, the beauty and delight of our ritual has only deepened.

FALL PRUNING

This is one of two annual prunings for almost everything, except most of the fruit trees, berries, and roses. For some plants, pruning old growth makes room for the new. When we prune away the branches that are not on the right path, we create the best channel in which to grow—the main path that provides the best flow of energy to allow for the greatest potential. Pruning is such an elegant art form!

WORKING IN THE AUTUMN GARDEN—FALL PLANTING

Autumn and spring are the busiest times of the year in the garden. In Southern California, even after the harvest is finished and the garden cleaned up, there is pruning and fall planting to do.

Foremost in fall planting are the bulbs. Refrigerate tulip bulbs for four to six weeks to simulate the cold of winter if you're in a warmer zone; other bulbs can simply be planted. For the best effect, plant them in drifts of one type of bulb. This can be done in two ways: either digging a big trench and setting the bulbs in their places, then covering them with soil; or by planting them individually. Either way, come spring, you will feel your efforts were well spent!

The lovely, highly fragrant paperwhite narcissus is one of the bulbs that naturalize in Southern California. Commonly thought of as a spring flower, mine, which have been in the ground for many years, began blooming before Halloween.

In my gardener's heart and mind, it is also time to plant my favorites: pansies, stock, snapdragons, ornamental kale, nemesia, and primrose (English, fairy, and Obconica), foxglove, delphinium, larkspur, and linaria. Seeds for sweet peas, wildflowers, sugar snap peas, and snow peas are planted now, too. This timing is for gardens with mild winters. If you live in a cooler climate, you may not be able to plant until spring. Everything in the garden depends on the weather.

OPPOSITE: Fall colors behind Peter's Train Garden. A bonsai Japanese maple (left), bonsai Ginkgo biloba (right), and the Chinese pistache (background).

AWAKENING THE INNER GARDEN IN AUTUMN

How do you feel when you first notice the slight chill in the air and see the deciduous trees begin to change colors and drop their leaves? Undoubtedly, just as we have experienced many autumns in nature, we are also given a season of change in our human lives—the season of aging. Hopefully, we have developed—or can—a perspective that allows us to appreciate and perhaps celebrate these inevitable changes of life. In the inner garden, autumn is a time to prepare for old age. Just as we do a complete cleanup in our actual garden, this is a time for pruning and weeding and getting rid of what doesn't grow well or work in the garden of the heart.

Our autumn years offer an opportunity to examine our attachments to how we see the world. In both the inner and outer gardens, autumn is a time of letting go. Like the leaves that become the compost to nurture new growth, there are chemical changes in us.

In the inner garden, this is also time for financial responsibility—for looking at resources we will need for winter (old age). It's a time of budgeting, looking at habits, and making changes. This is not about deprivation or denial, but rather cleaning, weeding, and reorganizing our inner garden so we can enjoy the beauty of winter. To simplify, it is necessary to weed out and get rid of so much stuff—cleaning out closets, shelves, and drawers. Don't just move stuff around; take the time to let things go and say goodbye to them! In composting, it is important not to put plants that have gone to seed onto the pile. Similarly, in inner work, don't spread your weeds so they come back. There is great satisfaction in pulling weeds, especially when you get the roots; if not, you know the weed will return. When finished, one of the most rewarding aspects of garden work in autumn is appreciating the cleanliness and orderliness of the garden.

HOLDING ON AND LETTING GO

Teachings of impermanence abound in our gardens: Plants die; pests—anything from aphids to gophers—invade and, of course, there is unpredictable weather. So much of our garden and our lives depends on the weather and the availability of water.

Autumn is one of the most beautiful times of the year because of the changes, and yet in our lives, we are often resistant to and so afraid of change. There is beauty in every season and every time of life. No one teaches us how to age and still be a gardener. In my own experience, I have found it necessary to change my expectations. And much of this lesson has to do with letting go—again and again. The challenge is to meet the changes of aging with humor, grace, lightness of being, and a sense of wonder. In the garden, as in life, letting go of our regular habits and desires allows us time to pay attention to what is. And what is, for many of us, is that we just can't do what we used to be able to do, and as difficult as that may be, we must honor that.

This glorious season, though, is a time for harvesting the fruits of your experience, for looking deeply within and finding the courage to face your deepest feelings. It is the beginning of transformation, having the potential, as caterpillars do, of making a cocoon, going inside, and emerging into a new life as a beautiful butterfly. This is a precious season of nurturing your inner soul being.

IN APPRECIATION OF THE WISDOM OF AGING

I remember standing in the center of a rose bed while it was in full bloom. I was deadheading the roses and just stopped and stood there, taking in the beauty that surrounded me. One of the things I noticed was the activities of the bees. Bees know and value Old Roses that have almost finished their lives but still have much to offer. Bees are still attracted to the center (or soul) of aging roses, inspiring me to write this poem.

THE *Bees Know*

Roses, Roses, Roses . . .
Surrounded by Roses
Dripping and cascading
From arbors, arches, fences,
rooftops.
Those overhead
Rain down the Blessings
Of their petals
Upon me and around me.

Sweet, soft, sensuous . . .
Magnificent in their innocent
beauty,
Opening from buds,
Merging and emerging into
life.

Opening even more,
Their inner beauty so obvious.
Each so unique
Eventually reaching their peak.

But is that peak in their youth?
The Bees know.
Given their choice
Of a whole bush full of roses,
Guess which ones the Bees
visit first?
It's the aging roses.
Imagine that!

They choose to visit the roses
Shortly before their petals
shatter—
Right before their body falls
away
And they change form.

The Bees are eager
To visit these old beauties—
Eager to learn of their secrets.

A Bee enters a rose.
Contentedly then ecstatically,
The Bee explores the wonders
Of the inner rose.

Drinking deeply of her treasures.
Then the Bee emerges—
Drunken with Love.

From The Garden · To The Kitchen

Most Delicious
PERSIMMON-DRIED APRICOT CHUTNEY

This chutney is a great addition to Indian food, veggies, dal, chicken, or meat. Because this chutney is so popular, we make a very large batch using three large pots and two canners, so feel free to size up the recipe depending on how many persimmons you have.

FOR THE CANNING

1 canner

4 (8-ounce) Mason jars with lids and rings

Small pot, for boiling lids and rings

FOR THE CHUTNEY

6 cups chopped Fuyu (Japanese) persimmons

2¾ cups unsulfured dried apricots

2 cups unsulfured raisins

2 cups apple cider vinegar

2 cups dark brown sugar

2¼ teaspoons chili powder

1⅓ tablespoons mustard seed

2 teaspoons ground ginger

MAKES 4 (8-OUNCE) JARS

To prepare the canning jars

1. Follow the detailed General Canning Instructions on page 146.

To make the chutney

1. In one large pot over medium-high heat, combine the persimmons, apricots, raisins, vinegar, sugar, chili powder, mustard seed, and ginger and mix well. Bring to a boil, stirring often. Lower the heat to a simmer and cook, stirring often, until thickened, about 20 minutes.
2. Spoon the chutney into the prepared jars, leaving ¼-inch headspace. Wipe the rims of the jar clean with a paper towel or kitchen towel. Top with the lids and screw on the rings.
3. Return the sealed jars to the canners and bring the water to a boil over medium-high heat. Boil for 10 minutes.
4. Remove the jars from the canner and place them on kitchen towels. Listen for the *pop, pop, pop,* indicating your jars have properly sealed.

GARDEN AND KITCHEN OF
LITTLE ACRE

From The Garden To The Kitchen

Chunky
CINNAMON APPLESAUCE

This is the easiest multi-purpose treat. Add it to oatmeal, use it as a topping for cakes, mix it into yogurt, or even add it to cooked rice and plain yogurt for rice pudding! I like to use Granny Smith apples, but you may choose to use a variety. I suggest using at least half Granny Smith, though. Red apple peel also adds a lovely color. I do not peel the apples because I like the rustic texture.

FOR THE APPLESAUCE

4 pounds apples of your choice

1 to 2 tablespoons ground cinnamon

FOR THE CANNING (OPTIONAL)

Canner

4 (8-ounce) Mason jars with lids and rings per each canner

Small pot, for boiling lids and rings

MAKES 4 (8-OUNCE) JARS

To make the applesauce

1. Wash the apples, remove the cores, and cut them into chunks.
2. In a large pot, sprinkle 1 tablespoon of cinnamon over the apples. Add more, if you really like cinnamon.
3. Add ½–1 inch of water to the bottom of the pot. If you add too much, you will have watery applesauce.
4. Cover the pot and bring to a simmer over medium heat. Cook, stirring often, until the apples are soft. Spoon the applesauce into jars and refrigerate for up to 1 week, or, if you prefer to can the applesauce, see the following instructions.

To can the applesauce (optional)

Refer to pages 146 for canning instructions. Properly sealed applesauce will last for up to 12 months.

WINTER

BARE *Roots*, BARE *Bones*

Winter is the season for planting bare-root plants, such as roses, some fruit trees, and vines. It is also the time of year when the "bones" of the garden, or its structure—the shapes of many deciduous trees, roses, vines, hedges, patios, walls, fences, and pathways—are visible.

It is a fallacy to think that winter is a full season of rest in the garden. I make a point of finishing all garden work the week before Thanksgiving here in the U.S., because once the holidays arrive, there are other priorities. So that means bulbs planted, fall pruning and planting finished, and the garden thoroughly cleaned up. Harvesting of persimmons and pomegranates will continue into the winter. Until it is time for pruning the roses (which, in Southern California, is after Christmas through February, weather permitting), there is no need to work in the garden. So, the "resting time" in my garden starts right before Thanksgiving and continues until after Christmas, and includes any rainy days. And as the garden rests, it is time for the gardener to rest as well.

But by the middle of December, my hands get a certain restless feeling. They anticipate the joy of pruning roses. Don't get me wrong: It is work, too! But also, gratifyingly fun. Pruning roses forces them to rest, and in areas of snow or cold weather, it protects them. Southern California is not one of those areas, so I modify the standard for rose pruning. I prune Hybrid Tea roses thigh high and floribundas knee high, and everything else I cut back by one-third.

My favorite part of hands-on gardening is pruning roses. Pruning roses encourages new growth and is like setting an intention for the future. It is one of the best meditative practices I know. When I prune roses, I am totally present with each rose, thinking only about how and where to prune. For that time, those moments, nothing else exists. And when all the pruning is finished, I so enjoy looking at the resting winter garden, feeling like I have helped my roses manifest fully. I see this bare garden as full of potential and have the faith to believe that these sticks with thorns will transform themselves into a beautiful garden when the season is right.

Each winter, one plans—even dreams about—what to include in next season's garden. Seed catalogs abound with new plants to grow. Some of us draw garden plans, keep careful records, and order specific plants; others just go and see what looks good at the nursery. Both ways work.

> *"The temple bell stops,*
> *but the sound keeps coming*
> *out of the flowers."*
>
> —BASHO

AWAKENING THE INNER GARDEN IN WINTER

In the inner garden, winter is a time for inner reflection and transformation. For most of us, our daily lives are busy attending to basic needs—our own and those of our family. Busy as we are, we often overlook the importance of setting aside quiet time, and we fail to prioritize unscheduled time just for ourselves. I'm talking about the kind of time that will bring us into the moment and provide us with love, peace, and a connection to the Source—time to reside within our soul.

Winter is time for letting go of what is not possible for you to do, what you may never do again in this lifetime, or what you had and lost. There may be grief associated with this. Try to see yourself without judging. Develop compassion for yourself. Allow yourself to show your vulnerability so people will really know you. Follow nature's way, withdrawing to journey within. Cultivate self-trust and self-love. Take refuge in your soul.

I invite you to be willing to be with the emptiness of winter—to make space for the unique manifestation of the divine beauty in each of us.

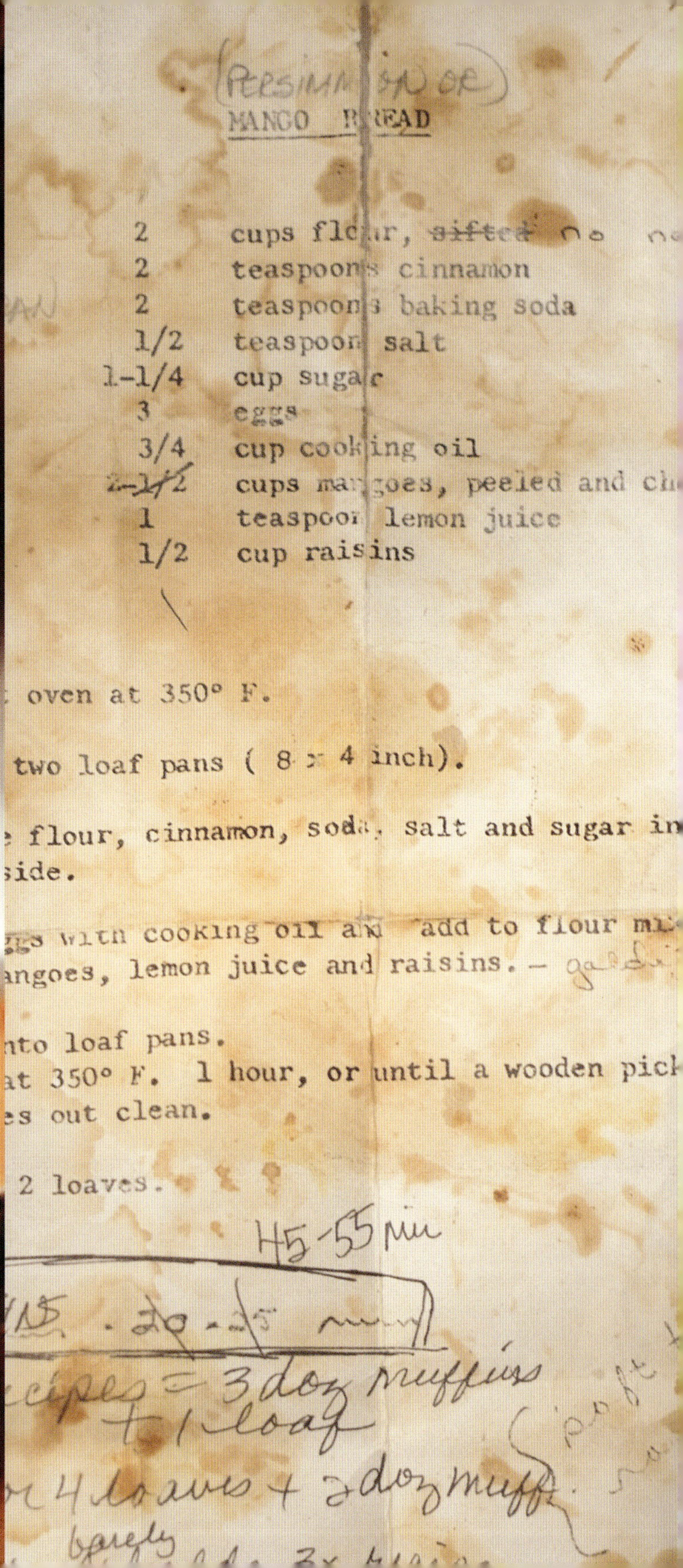

(PERSIMMON OR)
MANGO BREAD

2	cups flour, ~~sifted~~ no
2	teaspoons cinnamon
2	teaspoons baking soda
1/2	teaspoon salt
1-1/4	cup sugar
3	eggs
3/4	cup cooking oil
~~2-1/2~~	cups mangoes, peeled and ch
1	teaspoon lemon juice
1/2	cup raisins

oven at 350° F.

two loaf pans (8 x 4 inch).

e flour, cinnamon, soda, salt and sugar in
side.

ggs with cooking oil and add to flour mi
angoes, lemon juice and raisins.

nto loaf pans.
at 350° F. 1 hour, or until a wooden pick
es out clean.

2 loaves.

45-55 min

ins . 20-25 min

ecipes = 3 doz muffins
+ 1 loaf

r 4 loaves + 2 doz muff

From The Garden To The Kitchen

Sandy's
PERSIMMON BREAD

A Christmas favorite! I make many dozens of muffins to share for gifts. My friends at the nursery started asking me in October when the persimmons will be ripe. And in the summer, I substitute mangos for persimmons. Delicious!

2 cups all-purpose flour

2 teaspoons ground cinnamon

2 teaspoons baking soda

½ teaspoon salt

1¼ cups sugar

3 eggs, at room temperature

¾ cup cooking oil

2 cups persimmon pulp (see Note)

1 teaspoon lemon juice

½ cup raisins

MAKES 2 (9-BY-4-INCH) LOAVES OR 18 TO 24 STANDARD-SIZE MUFFINS

1. Preheat the oven to 350°F. Grease two 9-by-4-inch loaf pans or line two 12-cup muffin tins with paper liners.
2. In a large bowl, combine the flour, cinnamon, baking soda, salt, and sugar. Set aside.
3. In the bowl of a stand mixer, combine the eggs and cooking oil and beat until well mixed. Add the flour mixture and beat on low just until fully mixed. Add the persimmons, lemon juice, and raisins and beat on low until incorporated.
4. Divide the batter equally between the two loaf pans. Bake for 1 hour, or until a toothpick inserted into the center comes out clean. If baking muffins, fill the cupcake liners ⅔ full. Bake for 20 to 25 minutes, or until a toothpick inserted into a muffin comes out clean.
5. Let cool on a wire rack for 10 minutes, then remove the cakes from the loaf pans or the muffins from the cupcake tins and let cool completely.

Note:

To make pulp from Hachiya persimmons, let them ripen until they have the consistency of a marshmallow. Cut the persimmons in half, scoop out the pulp, and discard the skin. If you are not going to use the pulp immediately, place the pulp in a Mason jar and squeeze a little lemon juice on top. Cover the jar with the lid and refrigerate for up to 3 days. You can also freeze for up to 6 months, but leave 1 inch of headspace to allow the pulp to expand. Do not tighten the lid when freezing; leave loose enough to jiggle.

BRINGING IT HOME

Garden Practice

ADD AGED CHARM TO A YOUNG GARDEN

Usually, it takes years—many changes of the seasons—for a garden to look and to feel "established." There is a certain *je ne sais quoi* in a mature garden. Perhaps that has to do with the years of tender, loving care—it has soul.

While these suggested shortcuts might not fully capture a garden with many years of loving, sometimes we just can't wait—especially for us older folks, or people that have moved and are starting over, or those who have a chronic or terminal diagnosis. In any case, creating a garden, any garden, will nourish the gardener. And why not make it charming?

- Buy the largest plants you can afford, at least a few of them.
- Plant fast-growing vines such as white solanum, honeysuckle, passion vine, climbing roses, rambling roses, wisteria, or jasmine.
- Use garden antiques, like planters, furniture, or wheelbarrows.
- Whenever possible, use natural-aged materials such as old wood, used brick, twigs, and branches when building anything in the garden (like structures, walls, pathways, etc.).

PHOTOGRAPH YOUR GARDEN

I invite you to take photographs of your garden, as well as close-ups of individual flowers. It may allow you to see, know, and understand your garden in different ways. Photos also give you a more intimate relationship with your flowers.

OPPOSITE: 'Alchymist' (Climber, 1956) growing on the stone pillar at the walk-in entrance to Gaals' Little Acre. ABOVE: An arrangement of 'Alchymist' blooms.

BRINGING IT HOME

Spiritual Practice

MAKING FRIENDS WITH CHANGE

It seems like much of life, especially as we age, has to do with letting go and making friends with change, and hopefully, being able to do so with grace and ease.

Ram Dass often said, "Make friends with change." Reflect about death and become friendly with it. Tune back into nature so you can feel the cycles of which you are a part. The process of aging is itself a creative act. When you are creating from peace, equanimity, and quiet the spaciousness of being in love with the Universe, you become a wise elder in the society.

WABI SABI AND MONO NO AWARE

It is so true that "beauty is in the eyes of the beholder." Beauty is a subjective quality, different for each individual. It can also be a cultural perception. I had a deep intuitive appreciation for the elements of *wabi sabi* and *mono no aware* (pronounced ah-WAH-ray), even before I knew there were names for these important components of Japanese aesthetics and culture.

The term *wabi sabi* initially referred to the qualities of a contemplative life, often lived in solitary existence surrounded by nature, with appreciation for spiritual values and the aesthetics of the natural world. The poet Basho used the term to explain the moments in life that were both lovely and lonely. It describes the delicate marvel of things like snowflakes and the surprising happiness one might find in giving away a precious item. The term eventually came to mean a celebration of the beauty of something aged by time—be it living beings or objects, with all their rich character and imperfections.

Basho also coined the phrase *mono no aware*, which meant a sensitivity and emotional receptivity to life in a solitary and sorrowful way. Both *mono no aware* and *wabi sabi* express a sensitivity to loneliness and solitude, but Basho used *mono no aware* to describe the resulting progression to sorrow, while *wabi sabi*, in contrast, refers to a contemplative mind that embraces imperfection. This beauty tinged with sadness includes an acceptance of the sorrows of life and the finite nature of things.

You will find the concepts of wabi sabi and mono no aware will enrich your life and help you value Mother Nature and your garden. They can transform feelings of judgment into an appreciation of beauty and value: the crack or chip in your favorite planter or pot; the spot that has been worn away by time on fabric or furniture; the patina, uneven surfaces, crackling, and changes in color that come with time—like sand dollars; the inevitable wrinkles on an aging face; and your deepest feelings and emotions. We can see all these as flaws or as the beauty of aging and change.

PRACTICE GRATITUDE

Practice gratitude—for things big and small. From the moment you wake up, before you start your day, listen with your quiet mind, not yet caught up in the events of the day.

If you begin and/or end the day at your puja table, you might light a stick of incense and read a few lines from a holy book, or *pranam*, and sit with your beloveds. It feels good to have a set time every day for this ritual.

In the shower, take time to anoint your body with a special soap or oil (I love rose-scented glycerine soap) and offer a prayer for the health of your body and its ability to be of service.

You might also want to keep a gratitude journal, making note each evening of the things you were grateful for that day.

And throughout the day, remember . . . and return to this inner space of love.

The Evolution of Soulful Sanctuaries

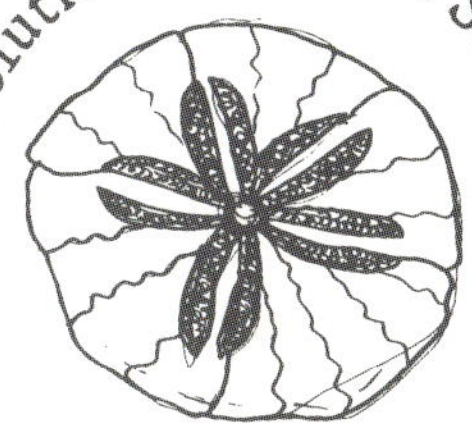

CHAPTER SIX

Gardening soothes our souls and revitalizes our spirits. There is joy and there is a sense of magic and hope that dreams really do come true. Gardens provide inspiration for others to create their own garden dreams.

"In the garden of memory, in the palace of dreams . . .
that is where you and I will meet."

—LEWIS CARROLL, *Alice Through the Looking Glass*

THE *Garden* OF THE *Heart*

The most important element you put into your garden is love. Still, the evolution of the soul of the garden is a continuous process, just as is our own spiritual evolution. It is a merging with that which you love. When you really quiet down, your sense of time changes or disappears. You become one with the flowers, the forms of the garden, the colors, the design, and the season—with each moment. The outer garden merges with the inner, bringing a sense of peace and joy and wonder. It is transformative.

There is always something new and fresh when exploring the miracles and changes that occur every day in the garden. I can't help but feel that my daily wanderings on the paths—deadheading here, noting changes in growth or things that need attention there, and just embracing the beauty—let the garden know it is cherished and valuable. What being would not flourish, knowing this? With time, your garden will teach you to trust your instincts, have faith, stay open, pay attention, and have patience. Enjoy the process.

Gaals' Little Acre Is FOR *Sale*

Once upon a time there was a garden. It was a much-loved garden. For the purpose of the garden was to bring joy and peace and beauty and imagination and a connection to nature and to the Divine. And because it was so loved, the garden had a soul.

After Peter's death, it became clear to me: I had to sell Gaals' Little Acre. It was just too much to handle. Had I really been listening, I would have sold it several years earlier, but the emotional attachment to both home and garden and the associated connections to our life together was tremendous. When I allow my mind to reminisce, a flood of precious memories engulfs me. And I am grateful for those memories.

THE SORROW OF PARTING

Even after 50 years of spiritual practice, saying goodbye to the physical presence of a beloved involves a whole realm of suffering and loss that words just cannot capture. It doesn't matter how old they are or how ready they are to leave their bodies. What does help is that we don't want them to suffer. Yet, even realizing this, there is a certain sorrow that lingers forever. Yes, it comes and goes, and yes there is acceptance, and yes, we continue on, and yes, we will be happy again; yet the world will never be the same and that sorrow of parting becomes part of who we are.

To be with anyone at their time of transition is a sacred honor. From my experience as an ICU nurse, I know that, without a doubt, there is a palpable time when the soul leaves the body. It is the feeling that the person is no longer present. And it is a feeling of peace.

Buddhist teacher Frank Ostaseski, co-founder of Zen Hospice in San Francisco and a most beautiful soul, says, "Before we can let go, we must let in." He is referring to letting in grief. He further explains, "Grief is the way we love a person. Grief is love that has no place to go." We don't just lose our beloveds once, but over and over again as memories remind us, even happy memories. And grief has no timetable. It must run its course, and that is different for everyone.

My spiritual practices were doorways into deeper connections, which manifested in the gardens I created and the way in which I shared them, as well as the inner changes I experienced and their reflections in my worldly life. When I look back on my life, I see that the goal of life is about becoming love. It's all a spiritual practice—compassion, gratitude, grace, living with faith. The joys and sorrows, the sufferings and grace, the loving, living, and dying we encounter in life give our hearts songs to sing—songs that uncover who we are as souls, songs that let us know our inner strength in the face of adversity, songs that can awaken our connection with the Divine. Everything is part of the design of this incarnation, to help each of us manifest fully.

A NEW LIFE

Somewhere along the way, I did let go of my garden. It took years for the sense of missing it to lessen; for the anger to subside at hearing of each healthy, productive tree or rose that had been ripped out of the ground; and every change in the beauty I had created in our home. It was no longer mine. I had to let go.

An amazing series of events helped ease the pain and grief. On a visit with close friends and Ram Dass in Maui, someone mentioned a listing that had just been posted for the rental of a small cottage five minutes away from Ram Dass's home. I checked it out online. It had a beautiful view! I called the landlord and told him I would take it without even seeing it in person and would be right over. It was a gigantic leap of faith! But I followed my heart and one thing after another just fell easily into place. The years I have lived there changed my life in ways I never dreamed possible.

I strongly believe in following one's heart. This is closely related to listening to your intuition. It may not make sense to you initially. It may be helpful to develop a dialogue between your heart and your head. But ultimately, I would always choose to have the faith to follow my heart.

"Happiness is when what you think, what you say, and what you do are in harmony."

—MAHATMA GHANDI

"The Soul cannot thrive in the absence of a garden."

—SIR THOMAS MORE, *Utopia*

Nature AS A *Refuge*

When I live with the conscious awareness of my soul, my heart is filled with love. The soul is always there, but sometimes it is hidden. The question then becomes how to get in touch with that tender part of you that can recognize, relate to, and act from your spiritual heart. And from that awareness, how do you visualize, manifest, and nurture both the inner and outer aspects of your being?

In every facet of life, we will have joys and sorrows. When faced with sorrows, spending time in the garden or in other natural surroundings can be very healing. In times of pain and suffering, just as a mother is there to comfort a small child, Mother Nature is always waiting to provide solace. My potager, the section of our orchard with roses, veggies, and herbs, did not have any spiritual statues. Yet, as I approached the arbor covered by the rose 'Cl. Pinkie' (which is almost always in bloom) and saw the view of the garden beyond—it took my breath away.

Silence and receptivity are integral elements in evoking the creative process and connecting to your soul. When you are in a garden—really, fully with a garden—you quiet down. Your mind quiets down and becomes more one-pointed, more focused on the beauty of nature. Becoming quiet allows you to make that transition into your heart, into your soul, into the love that lives within you. A garden is such a wonderful vehicle for getting to this heavenly place. The soul of a garden is love. And the soul blossoms in the presence of such beauty.

May there always be a garden in your life. May it provide you with joy and a sense of wonder and teach you nurturing and patience. May you learn that when you put your love into something, you discover the love that lives within you, and that love becomes palpable and evokes a feeling of inner peace. May it be your connection to knowing that you are part of nature, part of the Universe and Universal Spirit. May the beauty of nature permeate your life.

"If I were to give people one instruction I would say:
Work on yourself.
Have compassion for yourself.
Allow yourself to be beautiful
And all the rest will follow."

—RAM DASS

BRINGING IT HOME
Garden Practice

EMBRACE THE BEAUTY OF NATURE

Find a comfortable place to sit in your garden or a beautiful place in nature. Embrace the beauty. Inhale its essence. Feel love flowing through you. Immerse yourself in that love. When you tune in to the wellspring of love within, your life becomes your path. Share it with each being you meet. Make every moment precious.

I have found that working in the garden (especially deadheading), watching the sunset, becoming one with the clouds, being with the ocean, walking or hiking, and appreciating the beauty of nature in her many flowered costumes can all be quieting in a meditative way.

While relaxing on the beach or cloud-gazing, journey within and discover the beauty of the divine self that you are—that each living creature is: a unique expression of The One.

The heart of nature is a state of peace.

BRINGING IT HOME

Spiritual Practice

ABOVE: This is Jizu, the Buddha who watches over children and women. He stood near our front door.

KARMA YOGA AND DHARMA

In *Paths to God, Living the Bhagavad Gita*, Ram Dass defines karma yoga as "the path of action. The practice of consciously using one's daily life and work as a spiritual path, while relinquishing attachment to the fruits of the actions."

Dharma is the spiritual way of living your life—the way that best keeps the world in harmony and moves you toward spiritual awareness. Karma is what you are given to do in your life, based on past actions. Doing something with the intention of making it a spiritual practice, of using it to go to God, is what makes it yoga. It is the intent and manner of doing something that characterizes the action—not the act itself.

The karmic path is different for each individual. Anyone who is devoted to their work or profession, and through that work provides a service to others, can technically be defined as a karma yogi. The service of karma yoga need not be restricted to one's work or profession. Anyone, by the way in which they treat others, can be of service, because there are no "others." When we deal with people with our full presence, respect, kindness, and love, we are being of service.

I invite you to spiritualize your life. Use all the events of your life as a pathway—a possibility of merging with the Universe. Sacredness is everywhere.

Remember the precious moments.
Look for the grace.

NAMASTE

In India, when people meet and part, they say "Namaste," which means:

I honor the place in you
Where the entire universe resides,
I honor the place in you
Of love, of light, of truth, of peace.
I honor the place in you
Where if you are in that place in you and
I am in that place in me
There is only one of us.

From The Garden To The Kitchen

Ram Dass's Favorite
DUTCH APPLE CAKE

Many times over the years, Ram Dass told me how much he loved this cake. One birthday, he had five beautiful cakes on the table. When someone asked him which cake was his favorite, without hesitation he pointed to the Dutch Apple Cake I had baked.

3 eggs

½ cup plain yogurt

½ cup canola oil

1 teaspoon vanilla extract

2 cups plus 2 teaspoons sugar

2 cups all-purpose flour

1 teaspoon baking soda

3 teaspoons ground cinnamon, divided

4 cups Granny Smith apples (5 to 6 apples), peeled and roughly chopped into chunks

MAKES 1 CAKE

1. Preheat oven to 350°F. Lightly oil a 9-by-13-inch baking dish.
2. In a large bowl, mix together the eggs, yogurt, canola oil, and vanilla until well mixed.
3. In a medium bowl, combine the 2 cups sugar, flour, baking soda, and 2 teaspoons cinnamon.
4. Transfer the dry ingredients into the wet ingredients and mix well. Add the apples and mix well. Pour the batter into the baking dish.
5. In a separate small bowl, mix together the remaining 1 teaspoon cinnamon and remaining 2 teaspoons sugar. Sprinkle the mixture evenly over the batter.
6. Bake for 50 to 60 minutes, or until a toothpick inserted into the cake comes out clean. Let cool for at least 15 minutes before cutting into squares and serving.

TOP 10 ROSE LISTS

FROM MY *Favorite Rosarians*

I am proud to call the rosarians featured here my friends. Each of them is extremely knowledgeable about roses and shares his or her passion for roses freely. They all devote a generous amount of time to educating and encouraging all who express an interest in the joy of growing roses. Many of these rosarians also design rose gardens. It was as difficult for these rosarians to list only 10 of their favorite roses as it was for me to include only 10 rosarians!

MICHAEL MARRIOTT

Michael has the enviable job of traveling to see gardens all over the world. He worked with David Austin Roses for over 35 years. During this time, he has designed private rose gardens and prestigious public gardens in many different countries. Michael recently published the beautiful book *Roses: An Inspirational Guide to Choosing and Growing the Best Roses*. And inspirational it is!!

I've always been passionate about plants and gardens and was brought up in France with a little garden of my own.

In 1985, I became nursery manager at David Austin Roses. Since then, my job and the nursery has changed hugely from a small, barely known nursery that had just introduced Graham Thomas to the much larger and well-known nursery it is today.

From knowing very little of roses, I now know a lot more, and over the past few decades have spent much of my time designing rose gardens, writing, and talking about them, being the main source of knowledge on all things relating to roses at the nursery, and generally trying to persuade people that roses are wonderful in all sorts of different ways. While they are obviously special plants, I try to encourage a commonsense way of growing them and very much encourage selecting the right rose for the right position accompanied by good soil preparation and management.

Here is my list of 10 favorites, bearing in mind that this is in the UK, although they are generally varieties that do well in most climates—except perhaps the hottest. In choosing roses, it is always important to consider the whole plant, not just the bloom. —M.M.

1. **'Munstead Wood'** (English, 2007) The best of the red English Roses with very beautiful, very double, dark red flowers and the most superb, rich, fruity Old Rose fragrance. Very good compact growth.

2. **'Francis E. Lester'** (Rambler, 1946) The ramblers are a wonderful group, and this is one of the very best. The flowers are soft pink and dog-rose-like with five petals. The strong fragrance is the classic musk rose type that wafts on the wind. These are followed by small orange hips that last well into the winter and are beloved by birds. A particularly tough and reliable rose.

3. **'Queen of Denmark'** (OGR, 1826) Many of the Old Roses have so much character and this one particularly so. The flowers are perfectly shaped, of the purest pink, and have a very strong, pure Old Rose fragrance. It is the grey green leaves setting off the pink petals that make it such a worthwhile choice.

4. **'Lady of Shalott'** (English, 2009) This rose is outstanding for its ability to produce seemingly endless quantities of flowers well into winter. They are not the classically shaped, very double blooms of many English Roses, but still very beautiful and a lovely shade of apricot. It's a tall, vigorous variety that can be grown as a shrub or climber.

5. **'Desdemona'** (English, 2015) To my mind, this is the best of the white English Roses. The flowers are medium size but produce extremely freely and have a strong, fruity fragrance that will fill a room if cut. It is

quite a compact shrub ideally suited to small borders but excellent, too, for growing in large pots.

6. **'The Generous Gardener'** (Cl. English, 2002) A really lovely climber. The flowers are soft pink, large, and not too double, with the most superb fragrance that is a mix of Old Rose, musk, and myrrh. If it is not deadheaded, large orange hips will form that last well into the winter. A particularly tough and reliable rose.

7. **'Gertrude Jekyll®'** (English, 1986) Certainly one of the best of the English Roses (indeed, any rose) for fragrance as well as sheer strength and quality. The flowers are particularly beautiful, too, very double and rosette shaped. It can be grown as both a shrub and a climber

8. **'Celsiana'** (Damask, before 1732) Most Old Roses have very double flowers, but Celsiana is one of the exceptions that proves the rule. They are semi-double with 12–15 pure pink petals that pale with age. It has a delightfully relaxed habit and a delicious damask fragrance.

9. **'Rosa setipoda'** (Wild Rose, 1899) There are many beautiful wild roses. *R. setipoda* is one of the best with fragrant, single flowers of soft pink fading with age and set off by graceful growth and attractive leaves. These are followed by red flagon-shaped hips that last well into autumn.

'Celsiana'

10. **'Hansa'** (Rugosa, 1905) The rugosas are known for being not only super healthy, but also extremely tough and reliable, and Hansa is no exception. The flowers are a strong, rich magenta and have a particularly powerful and delicious Old Rose fragrance. It sets a good crop of very large orange hips much loved by the birds.

CLAIR MARTIN

Clair Martin is an internationally renowned rosarian of many talents. In 1982, he became the curator of roses at The Huntington Botanical Gardens in Pasadena, California, supervising the care of over 2,000 species and cultivars of old and modern roses. He has written two wonderful books, *100 English Roses for the American Garden*, and *100 Old Roses for the American Garden.* Now retired from The Huntington, Clair remains one of the rose world's most esteemed rose experts.

Over my 40-year career in horticulture, I grew and observed many roses, but early on I began to focus on the older historic cultivars. It was a combination of their stories and how their names reflected human history. Authors and artists have told the story of the rose in writing and paint, and their work continues to have surprising contributions in our modern world. A collection of roses can tell the story of our wars, heroes, and loves. The history of roses is our history. —C.M.

1. **'Autumn Damask'** (Damask, before 1913) First mentioned by the Roman poet Virgil in 30 BCE, this is one of the few truly Old Roses that rebloom in mild climes.

2. **'Great Maiden's Blush'** (Alba, 1843) This is ancient and of a style popular in Flemish floral paintings. A large shrub that emits a heavenly scent.

3. **'Old Blush'** (China, circa 1752) This rose is the direct ancestor of our repeat blooming roses. She blooms repeatedly in mild climate gardens.

4. **'Slater's Crimson'** (China, 1790) This is the source of repeat blooming red roses. Having disappeared from gardens, this important parent was rediscovered in a garden in Bermuda.

5. **'Léda'** (Damask, 1827) This lovely, once-blooming rose starts as a crimson bud and opens to a blush pink with a red border that emits a lovely fragrance.

6. **'Tamora'** (English, 1983) I have planted this lovely apricot rose in many gardens. She repeats well and makes a wonderful display of her fragrant blooms.

7. **'Abraham Darby®'** (English, 1985) This is another of David Austin's early roses, with soft pink to apricot flowers with a powerful fragrance that is carried throughout the garden.

8. **'Double Delight'** (Hybrid Tea, 1976) Wonderfully fragrant roses with flowers composed of a swirl of cream, pink, and red. No two flowers are alike!

9. **'Mutabilis'** (China, pre-1894) Can only be described as a shrub covered in bright yellow flowers changing over the days to pink and ending crimson red.

10. **'Belle of Portugal'** (Cl. Tea, 1900) Her flowers are of a soft salmon pink. She is a big girl that loves to climb, with a lovely fragrance and flowers nodding down at admirers.

'Abraham Darby®'

BUD AND KAY JONES
SANTA BARBARA ROSE SOCIETY

On one of their visits to my garden, Bud and Kay gifted me with the beautiful rose 'Secret Garden Musk Climber,' which thrived in my Secret Garden and formed a "wall" separating it from the '60s Peace Garden.

We have been actively involved in growing roses since 1982 when we first attended a local rose society meeting. Currently we have about 120 bushes, downsized from at least 160 in the past, of all types from Hybrid Tea, floribunda, climbers, shrubs, OGRs, and minis. Our love of roses has brought us to local, nearby, district, national, and international shows and conventions, where we've met rose lovers from all over the world. Bud is an ARS horticultural judge, and we are both longtime consulting rosarians. —B.J. & K.J.

1. **'Altissimo'** (Climber, 1966) All red roses do not have to be many-petaled. This magnificent specimen has only five to seven petals, but what a show-off. With its vibrant yellow stamens and shiny green foliage. As it grows up a trellis, it holds its head up high for all to see and even rewards us with numerous sprays to behold.

2. **'Joasine Hanet'** (Damask Perpetual, 1847) Another "rescued" rose from the Gold Country of the California Sierras. The form is exquisite, as is the medium pink color and fragrance that jumps out at you. This rose is not easy to find, but if you can get one, you will be rewarded with great blooms and unique, fully quartered form.

3. **'Purple Splash'** (Climber, 2011) A vigorous climber by Tom Carruth. It is purple with white stripes and five to ten petals in clusters. Blooms all season.

4. **'Pookah'** (Polyantha, 2009) A recent addition to our garden is a light pink rose that blooms in clusters throughout the season. It was hybridized by our friend Jim Delahanty and has become one of our favorites.

5. **'Sally Holmes'** (Hybrid Musk Shrub, 1976) This plant has grown to very large proportions ranging out to six feet on each side and about eight feet high. It produces big clusters of creamy white flowers with an April appearance so thick with blooms you can hardly see the bush.

6. **'Mix 'N' Match™'** (Shrub, 1997) This is a shrub that is supposed to grow to 3 to 5 feet, but ours is easily 10 feet tall. It produces light pink flowers in large clusters covering the bush with occasional repeats later in the season.

7. **'Mel's Heritage'** (Hybrid Wichurana, 2011) Very vigorous with loads of pink blooms throughout the season. This plant grows up to eight feet tall by eight feet wide.

8. **'Molineaux™'** (English, 1994) Vigorous and disease resistant, this plant and produces many rich yellow blooms with the old garden look that keep well.

9. **'Graham Thomas®'** (Cl. English, 1983) Great yellow blooms borne of very long stems but we have tamed it down by cutting back to about four feet at the end of the season, resulting in many blooms that girdle the bush. This modern shrub has blooms that resemble the form and petal arrangement of Old Garden Roses.

10. **'Russelliana'** (Hybrid Multiflora, before 1837) A favorite for many reasons. We "rescued" this rose from an old, abandoned barn many years ago. When we planted it, we never realized it would grow so profusely and bloom its head off in the spring. It has fully double magenta blooms that are borne in clusters. Too bad it is not a repeat bloomer, as it is one of our favorites. Give it a lot of room.

'Sally Holmes'

CARRIE COOPER GRIFFITH
SANTA BARBARA ROSE SOCIETY

My involvement with roses began in the spring of 1988 when I moved from Los Angeles to Santa Barbara into a house with 13 or so rosebushes. I remember the varieties: 'Cynthia,' 'Love,' 'Cherish,' 'Gypsy,' 'Electron,' and 'Medallion,' to name a few. I was excited, then realized I didn't know how to care for them. The plants were thriving, and I wanted to be out in the garden with them. What made them tick? What did they need? I wanted to find out, so that summer I called the Santa Barbara Rose Society. I attended a meeting and have never looked back. —C.C.G.

1. **'Secret™'** (Hybrid Tea, 1994) Probably my favorite Hybrid Tea because it has it all—the cream bloom with the lovely pink edge and the fabulous Hybrid Tea form, with size to boot. But it is the fragrance that transcends; citrusy, rosy, and strong. To top it all off, it's vigorous and has a four-by-four-foot growth habit.

2. **'Royal Sunset'** (Cl. Hybrid Tea, before 1960) The first climber to bloom in my garden. The blooms have a deep burnt orangey-apricot color and the foliage is dark and leathery. The fragrance is grape/fruity and rose: divine. I love its quick repeat and abundance of bloom. For a climber, it can work nicely in a smaller garden, as it doesn't get huge.

3. **'Double Delight'** (Hybrid Tea, 1977) A Hybrid Tea I think every rose garden should contain. It has a contrasting cream center with a deep red edge. The fragrance signifies the beginning of spring to me—strong and rose. Not quite the vigor it used to have and prone to mildew, but it's still a rose that holds a place in my top 10.

4. **'Outta the Blue'** (Shrub, 2001) Love this shrub for its unique qualities: Magenta/purple with a yellow base and a spicy clove fragrance, it is vigorous and disease resistant and, most important, produces an abundance of blooms all over the plant. It does get tallish, but it has a roundness to it that I like.

5. **'Sombreuil'** (Climber, 1850) What a gorgeous, historical, large-flowered climber—creamy white with 100 petals, and full, flat form. I adore the myrrh fragrance, as well as its tall climbing habit. Its neutral color can be used in any garden. Canes, soft and pliable, can be trained easily over an arbor.

6. **'Fragrant Cloud'** (Hybrid Tea, 1967) Oh my! How I love the deep, salmon-pink color of this Hybrid Tea! The knock-your-socks-off scent is surpassed by none. I swoon each time I take a whiff. Not vigorous enough for me, and too prone to mildew—yet still a favorite.

7. **'Valencia'** (Hybrid Tea, 1987) Tommy Cairns showed a vase full of this lovely Hybrid Tea at a show and it was love at first sight! Then I smelled it—fabulous. A most unusual apricot cream, almost butterscotch. I love its compact habit and glossy foliage and wish it had a quicker repeat bloom.

8. **'Monsieur Tillier'** (Tea, 1891) It's all about the color and quartered form for me on this wonderful tea rose. I appreciate the classic burgundy laterals and tea fragrance. I also love its open, comfortable growth habit and rebloom.

9. **'Golden Celebration'** (English, 1992) I had a beautiful specimen of this shrub that I had to leave behind when I moved, and I miss it, especially the golden-yellow color and that distinctive David Austin fragrance. I love the full yet manageable growth habit—it needs room. A great yellow and a great David Austin!

10. **'Rosy Dawn'** (Miniature, 1982) Last, but not least, my first purchased rose from Dale Greer, our society president in 1989, who was moving and needed to reduce his rose numbers. I'd never seen anything like it—so small and white, with that deep pink edge. A fabulous little mini. Dark green foliage and so easy to grow. Just as exquisite in the bud as it is fully open.

'Double Delight'

JERI AND CLAY JENNINGS HERITAGE ROSE SOCIETY, VENTURA ROSE SOCIETY, SANTA BARBARA ROSE SOCIETY

Jeri and Clay Jennings have grown roses in coastal Southern California since 1987. The old once-blooming roses don't succeed in their climate, but tea roses and China roses *do*. They love OGRs for their beauty, their toughness, and their connection to history, and they have spent some time seeking out forgotten roses in old cemeteries and forgotten gardens in California. Jeri is the current national convenor and Clay is the membership chair for the Heritage Roses Group.

Jeri has also been president of several rose societies and has the honor of having roses named after her. When I was new to Ventura and first joined the Ventura Rose Society, it was Jeri who took me under her wing and encouraged my participation and sharing with fellow rosarians. These are her top 10 roses.

1. **'Grandmother's Hat'** (Hybrid Perpetual, 1972) My favorite rose, hands-down. In my coastal Southern California garden, this "found" rose is totally carefree. In our very rare warm-and-wet periods, it can black spot. But for the most part, it just sits there and grows and blooms. It was found first in Pasadena, California, by Fred Boutin, noting that it was so good it would probably be identified quickly. It was not. It was found again in the San Francisco Bay Area by the late Barbara Worl, who said the blooms reminded her of the pink silk roses on her grandmother's hats. Her study name stuck. No confirmed identification has ever been made, but this rose has been found in multiple locations in the Bay Area.

2. **'Secret Garden Musk Climber'** (Climber, before 1993) Offers great vigor, disease resistance, continuous bloom, and—most of all—an overwhelming musk fragrance. If single roses and fragrance attract you, this is definitely a rose you will want.

3. **'Mlle. de Sombreuil'** (Tea, 1851) This is a true tea rose, which blooms richly and continuously, in white or blush, altering with the seasons, and has magnificent disease resistance. This is a rose that was lost, and then replaced in commerce by a mid-20th-century climber of mysterious origin. We owe its rediscovery to Phillip Robinson, who found it in Santa Rosa, California, and was later able to correctly identify it. It was found again in a town 90 miles distant from Santa Rosa, on the grave of a young 19th-century blacksmith—George Washington Richardson.

4. **'Mel's Heritage'** (Hybrid Wichurana, 2011) Its breeder, Paul Barden, thought that this would be a once-blooming rambler-style climber. When he gave it to the San Jose Heritage rose garden to test it, 'Mel's Heritage' surprised everyone by turning out to be almost continuous-blooming—and blooming en masse! It is among the most fragrant roses I've ever grown, filling the air with rich fragrance through the year. And, oh, yeah, it's totally disease-free.

5. **'Lady Ann Kidwell'** (Tea, 1948) This seedling of 'Mlle. Cecile Brunner' was logically classed as a Polyantha. Vintage gardens included it in a small group of roses they identified as "Poly-Teas." I simply would call it a tea rose. Whatever you choose to call it, it is a vigorous, disease-free rose

that will grow tall, if allowed to. Blooms are best described as cerise in color and have the soft, rich character of thick satin bows. The nodding habit of the blooms is best appreciated if the plant grows above your head.

6. **'Benny Lopez'** (probable Bourbon, 2005) Growing beautifully on its own roots, this rose will form a large, arching shrub, which in California will bloom right through December. It is fragrant and great in a vase, but most important, it is a handsome shrub that adds beauty to any garden.

7. **'Old Town Novato'** (probable Hybrid Perpetual, 2003) This was found by Cass Bernstein at an old train station in Novato, California. Growing vigorously on its own roots, 'OTN' makes a gracefully upright shrub, which in a mild climate will bloom right through December.

8. **'Barbara's Pasture Rose'** (Hybrid Perpetual, before 2005) Sherri Berglund and the late Barbara Oliva went on a rose-hunting trip to the Gold Rush town of Cherokee, California. Leaving the old town, they passed a pasture (fortunately not tenanted at the time by cattle) surrounded by barbed wire fencing and containing a massive rosebush in full bloom.

   Barbara said, "Hold the wire. I'm going in." And so, 'Barbara's Pasture Rose' was collected. Think of this rose as "La Reine-on-Steroids"—just like 'La Reine' (1842) but larger in every way, and disease-free.

9. **'G. Nabonnand'** (Tea, 1888) The Nabonnands bred tea roses around the time when Hybrid Teas were gaining favor, so some of their roses straddle the line between the two. 'G. Nabonnand,' however, is "all tea" in its character—bushy, graceful habit, and generous production of pink/white clusters of bloom. It's also "all Nabonnand," in its complete disease resistance.

10. **'Mme. Lambard'** (Tea, 1878) This must surely have been the single most popular rose—certainly the most popular tea rose—in 19th-century California. Old, old plants are found in almost all old cemeteries and deserted gardens, surviving with a flare, where other roses failed and died. In my conditions, it will mildew from time to time, but it is the rose I can almost always count on for vases, right through the year.

'Grandmother's Hat'

SYL ARENA

Syl is a rosarian and owner of the former Arena Roses. For many years, he grew and sold beautiful, healthy roses and had the most beautiful rose catalog ever. His reputation for reliability and quality was dependable. Arena Roses was the only company in this country that I know of that also sold the Generosa roses of France's Guillot family.

1. **'Souvenir de la Malmaison'** (Bourbon, 1893) *soft pink.*

2. **'Mme. Joseph Schwartz'** (Tea, 1880) *white to light pink.*

3. **'Comte de Chambord'** (OGR, 1860) *light magenta.*

4. **'Rose de Rescht'** (Portland, 1840) *bright magenta.*

5. **'Paul Neyron'** (Hybrid Perpetual, 1869) *rose pink.*

6. **'Cornelia'** (Hybrid Musk, 1925) *light pink.*

7. **'Buff Beauty'** (Noisette, 1939) *apricot.*

8. **'Martine Guillot®'** (Shrub, 1997) *white/off-white.*

9. **'Sonia Rykiel'** (Shrub, 1991) *pink.*

10. **'Iceberg'** (Shrub, 1958) *white.*

'Comte de Chambord'

JEAN-PIERRE GUILLOT

What an honor to have Jean-Pierre Guillot, head of the number one rose-growing family in France, visit my garden! He is as charming a gentleman as the roses he has bred. His first visit was with Syl Arena. After that visit, I planted a new garden in his honor, containing six of his roses. On his second visit, his lovely wife, Martine, accompanied him. And on his third visit, he brought his own photographer!

1. **'La France'** (Hybrid Tea, 1867) *silvery pink.*

2. **'Dany Hahn®'** (Shrub, 2004) *white.*

3. **'Paul Neyron'** (Hybrid Perpetual, 1869) *rose pink.*

4. **'Martine Guillot®'** (Shrub, 1997) (no surprise!) *white/off-white.*

5. **'Emilien Guillot'** (Shrub, 2001) *orange-red.*

6. **'Comtesse du Cayla'** (China, 1902) *pink and yellow.*

7. **'Monique Bouygues'** (Shrub, 2010) *light pink with darker center.*

8. **'William Christie®'** (Shrub, 1998) *light pink.*

9. **'Etoile de Lyon'** (Tea, 1881) *deep yellow.*

10. **'Valérie de Montgolfier®'** (Floribunda, 2011) *orange-red.*

'Martine Guillot®'

DANIELLE DALL'ARMI HAHN

The lovely, creative, and knowledgeable Dani Hahn and her husband, Bill, created Rose Story Farm in Carpenteria, California. These beautiful gardens and successful rose business now are home to thirty thousand rosebushes with over 130 varieties.

In 2014, Dani was honored as the Great Rosarian of the World at The Huntington Botanical Gardens. The award was given for her significant contributions to the cultivation and appreciation of roses. She is also the author of the book *The Color of Roses: A Curated Spectrum of 300 Blooms*.

Bill and I both grew up in families that were wild about gardening, and our grandmothers on each side were rosarians. Bill was raised on a potato farm in central Washington, and some of the magical qualities of farming rubbed off on him. We chose to transform part of our lemon orchard into rose fields. Bill bulldozed hundreds of lemon trees, while I poured over rose books and catalogs to select my favorite one thousand rosebushes. Memories of my grandmother's fragrant roses inspired me to select mainly old-world roses with enticing scents. The farm is truly a family affair, and we find some of our best moments together, walking among and "working" the rows. Our roses bring us together to enjoy the simple pleasures of country life, and our family appreciates and savors the time we spend together caring for these exquisite flowers. —D.D.H.

1. **'Mme. Paul Massad'** (Shrub, 1997) *apricot.*
2. **'Martine Guillot®'** (Shrub, 1997) *white/off-white.*
3. **'Florence DeLattre'** (Floribunda, 1997) *mauve or purple blend.*
4. **'Sweet Mademoiselle™'** (Hybrid Tea, 2017) *pink.*
5. **'Fair Bianca®'** (Shrub, 1982) *white.*
6. **'Julia Child'** (Floribunda, 2004) *yellow.*
7. **'Love Song'** (Floribunda, 2011) *lavender.*
8. **'Papa Meilland'** (Hybrid Tea, 1963) *red.*
9. **'Bronze Star™'** (Hybrid Tea, 2000) *apricot.*
10. **'Pope John Paul II'** (Hybrid Tea, 2008) *white.*

'Florence DeLattre'

DAN BIFANO
SANTA BARBARA ROSE SOCIETY

Among his many talents, Dan has designed many awesome rose gardens, such as those he created for Lotusland, Oprah Winfrey, and Barbra Streisand. He is a longtime consulting rosarian, master rosarian, and rose judge.

I have always had roses in my life. My first memory of roses goes back about 65 years when we had six plants of the newly introduced 'Queen Elizabeth' in our garden. A short time later we moved to Montecito, and, before I was 10, I had a garden of 100 of the most popular Hybrid Tea roses of the day. Since then, I have continued to surround myself with roses. When I purchased my first home, it came with a half dozen but soon grew to more than 250. I began designing gardens in the late '80s for clients and continue to do so today.

I am a life member of the American Rose Society and a horticultural—as well as arrangement—judge, receiving many awards in these categories. Additionally, I am currently chair of the Advisory Counsel for Lotusland. I am also a master rosarian. I have been honored to have my work appear repeatedly on The Oprah Winfrey Show *and in* O, The Oprah Magazine. *My work has also been featured in* Veranda, Architectural Digest, *and, most recently,* Vogue. *I have had acknowledgments from David Austin and other notable rosarians and been included in Barbra Streisand's book* My Passion for Design. *—D.B.*

1. **'Carding Mill'** (English, 2004) *apricot.*

2. **'Princess Alexandra of Kent'** (English, 2007) *bright pink.*

3. **'Over the Moon'** (Hybrid Tea, 2005) *apricot.*

4. **'Lasting Love™'** (Hybrid Tea, 1993) *red.*

5. **'Koko Loko'** (Floribunda, 2010) *chocolate, lavender.*

6. **'Olivia Rose Austin™'** (English, 2014) *mid pink.*

7. **'Francis Meilland®'** (Hybrid Tea, 1996) *light pink.*

8. **'Love Song'** (Floribunda, 2011) *lavender.*

9. **'Grande Dame™'** (Hybrid Tea, 2009) *deep pink.*

10. **'In the Mood™'** (Hybrid Tea, 2007) *red.*

'Princess Alexandra of Kent'

BOB EDBURG

Bob was a lover of OGRs, master rosarian, great educator, writer, owner of Limberlost Roses in Southern California, which sold OGRs and rose books. When he moved to North Carolina, he started Ashdown Roses.

Bob wrote five volumes of the awesome *Encyclopedia of Antique Roses*, which, among endless amounts of rose knowledge, contained classic colored plates of OGRs by Redouté and others.

He was a big man with a deep, booming voice. I learned that he had been a Shakespearean actor—I can only imagine! He had a table at my rose events selling rose books and was a wealth of knowledge, delivered with charm. Bob died of cancer in 2015, but I am delighted to have this list he sent me in 2009.

As I have written in my Encyclopedia of Antique Roses, *my love for Antique Roses began in 1942, when my grandmother gave me four of the roses she called 'American Beauty' to take care of. I've grown Antique Roses ever since. As you might imagine, my list begins with the obvious. —B.E.*

1. **'American Beauty'** (Hybrid Perpetual, 1886) The roses my grandmother gave me were really 'Ulrich Brunner,' as I found out later. 'Madame Ferdinand Jamain' has also been sold as 'American Beauty,' and actually, I am quite fond of all three. I confess I have always preferred Hybrid Perpetuals to any other class, because they are a wonderful representation of the late 1800s Victorian opulence. Lush petals, overwhelming fragrance, and, generally, deeper rose, carmine, and crimson colorings create an irresistible flower.

2. **'Climbing Souvenir de la Malmaison'** (Cl. Bourbon, 1893) The climbing version of this is by far the best example of the beauty and elegance exhibited by this classic Bourbon shrub. Marvelous fragrance and a cupped look while progressing to its ultimately flat shape when fully opened make this rose a "must" for every lover of Old Garden Roses.

3. **'Yolande d'Aragon'** (Portland, 1843) I like this rose for its deep pink coloring, heavy fragrance, and typical OGR look, with its reflexed petals tightly packed from the center outward. As with any rose, when grown in an ideal location for the particular variety, it can be an outstanding specimen. My five-year-old plant in Van Nuys had arching and self-pegging canes, 10–12 feet long, with the blooms "roped on" all along each cane.

4. **'Deuil du Docteur Reynaud'** (Bourbon, 1862) This bush has climbing tendencies but can be a large shrub when well-managed. The French list the coloring as "cramois noir," or dark crimson, but in California it was a rose-raspberry color. Typical full, open, Bourbon look, with a sweet fragrance.

5. **'Sultan of Zanzibar'** (Hybrid Perpetual, 1876) I do not have this rose, nor have I ever seen a live plant in bloom, but 15 years ago, when I first saw it in a chromolithographed reproduction, I have wanted it. It's a beautiful deep-rose color, with many chiffon-like petals on a large flower, although the fragrance is reputed to be moderate.

6. **'General Gallieni'** (Tea, 1902) Without doubt, one of the finest tea roses in existence. In my California garden, it was six feet tall, very robust, and almost always loaded with heavy, tea-scented, medium-pink blooms, with creamy-looking centers and rather ragged-edged petals, which were a large part of its charm.

7. **'Souvenir de Pierre Notting'** (Tea, after 1895) A most beautiful flower, with tightly packed petals of a rich yellow—fragrant and well-behaved. A tidy shrub, slightly smaller than the usual tea-rosebush size, which is 8–12 feet. Long-lasting blooms are wonderful for cut flowers and bouquets.

8. **'Fortune's Five-Colored Rose'** (Tea, 1843) This rose first came to me from Clair Martin, of The Huntington, as a rose he had gotten from Bermuda, where it was called 'Smith's Parish.' Its chief attraction is the appearance of the colors white and deep pink, in five different combinations—pure white, white with one pink petal, pure pink, pink with one white petal, and, finally, a rose with both colors displayed in a solid fashion, separated from each other as though a line had been drawn using a ruler to divide the bloom. Light fragrance, but deserving of a place in every rose garden.

9. **'Mrs. RG Sharmin Crawford'** (Hybrid Perpetual, 1894) A typical Hybrid Perpetual, a sturdy large shrub, almost always in bloom, with large, fragrant, light pink and white flowers in profusion.

10. **'Vick's Caprice'** (Hybrid Perpetual, 1893) A "must have," if only for the light pink-and-white-striped flowers, unusual amongst Hybrid Perpetuals. Mine always went through five major blooming periods, neatly spaced out from early spring to late autumn. Hardy and erect—always an attention-getter.

'Mrs. RG Sharmin Crawford'

Additional GARDENING *Guidance*

I am not presumptuous enough to think that I have all the answers to your garden questions. Yet, I do have 50 years of organic gardening experience and would love to share what works for me. So I suggest that you first read the "recipe," as many of us do before cooking, and then tweak it here and there as you see fit. Follow your heart and do what feels right.

Realize that gardens come in all sizes. I used to have an amazing acre of gardens. Now I have a lovely tiny garden and grow only a few roses, veggies, and herbs in containers. Every time a rose blooms, it's cause for celebration. It is the love and attention you give your garden that will give it soul and nourish you. So do what you can and make it special. A small, simple garden is a beautiful thing.

"There is magic in the garden. I cannot create a daffodil in all its color and grace. No man can. I do not know how a daffodil is created. Yet each spring thousands and thousands of them are seen dancing in our gardens. There is law in the garden. It is the law of creation. If we follow that law, we deal in magic. We cannot see the stuff of which the daffodil is made, we need not care by what process it comes into being. If we take the dark brown bulb, plant it according to that law at the right time—we achieve a miracle."

—ROY E. BILES

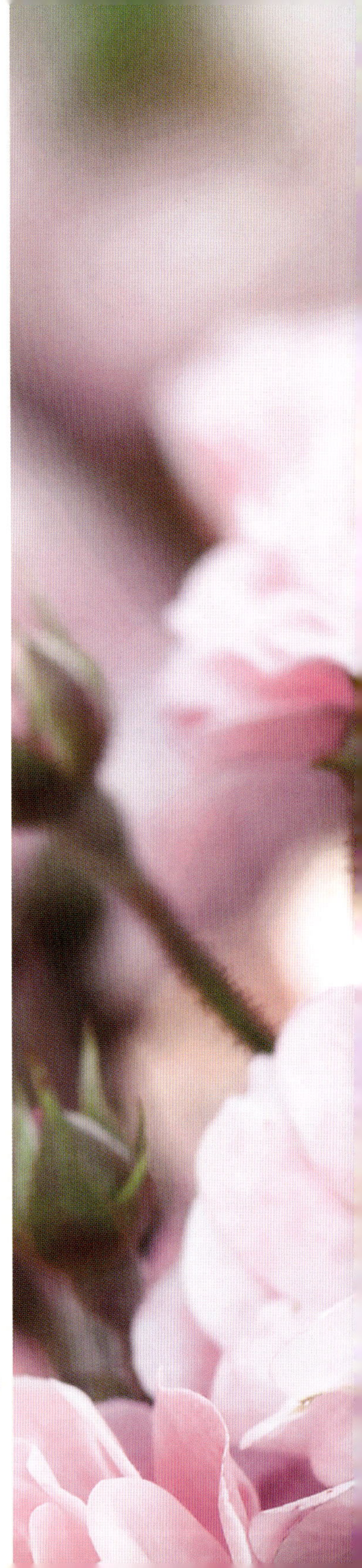

PEARLS OF GARDEN DESIGN

Decide on a shape. If a formal garden is what you want, you will need straight, geometrical edges, borders, or hedges. If you prefer a softer look and feeling, consider free-form beds. I prefer the latter or a combination of both. For example, if a bed with straight, classic boxwood borders, like a parterre, is planted with wildflowers, this will soften the straight edges and give you the best of both worlds. In creating a free-form bed, it helps to visualize your plan by laying out a garden hose to outline the area you have in mind.

It is my strong feeling that gardens need borders. Some would say gardens need ground covers, but I don't think it's necessary. To my eye, a border gives a garden a finished look. And they are fun! The fun comes in creating combinations of plants and colors that complement each other and make a statement. Just picture a bed or a container of herbs surrounded by yellow pansies or marigolds—much more interesting than only the herbs.

Plan for a water source. By this I mean you need a method for watering your garden. It could also mean a fountain or pond, but how you will water your garden is one of the most important decisions. Whenever possible, group plants with similar water requirements in the same area. Depending on the type of irrigation you choose, it is also possible to have different emitters in the same bed, which can deliver different amounts of water.

Design elements and themes. The vertical element adds such joy to a garden. Arbors, allées, pergolas, tuteurs, and pillars cascading with vines, roses, or flowers are delightful eye candy. They make the garden far more interesting, as do other focal points, such as a statue or vista framed by a hedge or arbor. On a smaller scale, upright plants of varying heights can add interest to garden beds.

If your space allows, garden rooms and theme gardens add a touch of whimsy and charm. Hopefully one of these spaces will have a transcendent, meaningful theme for you.

And if yours is a vegetable garden, grow what you love to eat. For fun, try to include something that you can pick and eat in the garden, like sugar snap peas, cherry tomatoes, or berries.

There are the classic beauties of rows and beds of veggies, but just think of how much fun it could be to make a design with your veggies by adding flowers—especially those that benefit their growth and decrease insects.

Right plant, right place. This is a concept of utmost importance. It does not matter how much you love roses, if all you have is deep shade, that just won't work. The plant may live, but it will not bloom. When deciding what you would like to grow, please learn the needs of each plant and honor them.

Color and sensual considerations. Color can set the feeling or mood of your space, and it is quite the personal preference when selecting them. I have a definite preference for not including orange and red most of the year in much of the garden, which is primarily an English/French cottage-style garden. Not very Hindu of me. I enjoy the bright colors in my summer garden, but usually prefer the more mellow shades of purples, maroons, dusty rose, pinks, blues, yellows, antique shades of tans/browns/cream, and always white. I am going for a peaceful feeling in the garden—and everywhere. In my

Japanese Garden and Garden of the Joyful Heart, if I included any flowers, they were white and usually azaleas. On the other hand, there is nothing as beautiful or sensuous as a classic red rose—but it must be a fragrant red rose. And for our bodies—a comfortable chair, love seat, chaise, or bench strategically placed, beckoning us to rest awhile and be with the garden.

Everyone has a garden within them. I trust you will have fun discovering yours.

FAVORITE PLANTS AND COMBINATIONS: HOW TO USE THEM IN THE GARDEN

Roses, roses, roses—you can never have too many roses! Try planting roses in shades of pink, burgundy, mauve, purple—and maybe a little tan—with a border of dwarf lavender (like 'Hidcote' or 'Munstead') or miniature roses (pink) or catmint (a lavender/blue flower). I would have to say that catmint is my favorite companion plant for my roses—especially roses in shades of pink and purple. Their blue color is such a beautiful complement. Planting foxglove in between the roses adds a lovely vertical accent and texture. It is toxic if eaten, though none of the eight dogs I have had have ever touched it.

- *Climbing roses with clematis* (which likes its feet in the shade and its head in the sun). I especially love 'Cl. Pinkie' (which blooms prolifically) with dark purple clematis. Pictured on page 3.
- *Yellow pansies with parsley* (and other herbs) This combination works well either as a border or interplanted. And perhaps include 'Johnny Jump Up' violas.
- *Purple ornamental kale* with purple and lavender sweet alyssum.
- *Ornamental kale*, white with a green edge, and 'Antique Shades,' as pictured below.
- *Coral bells* is grown primarily for its beautiful bronze foliage. I loved using this as the outside border around my two bronze urns that held topiaries, planting it in the center with 'Antique Shades' pansies, petunias, or 'Crystal Palace' lobelia.
- *Red oak leaf lettuce* can be used to surround rainbow Swiss chard. Perhaps add in some yellow pansies, violas, marigolds, or calendulas.

BORDER PLANTS

- *Germander* is a medicinal herb with a lavender-colored flower that makes a lovely border. Other border plants with lavender flowers are *brachycome* and thyme.
- *Lobelia*, also used as a trailing plant in window boxes or hanging baskets:
  - 'Crystal Palace' has bronze leaves and deep blue flowers.
  - 'Sapphire' is bright blue with a white "eye."
  - 'Cambridge Blue' has green leaves with powder blue flowers.
- *Perennial nemesia* comes in many beautiful colors.
- *Chrysanthemum paludosum* looks like a cluster of little white daisies.

CLIMATE CHANGE

Climate change is one of the most important issues of our time. It can't be ignored, and although the changes have been gradual, they may very well affect which plants will thrive in your garden. You will want to consider the direction these environmental changes seem to be taking in your area and factor them in the plantings you choose.

PLANTS THAT ADD THE ELEMENT OF HEIGHT AND CHARM TO THE GARDEN

❀ *Foxglove* is beautiful and self-propagates readily. Its leaves are used to make digitalis, which is a heart medication. It is toxic if eaten, though.

❀ *Lupine*. If you love lupine, I suggest reading the children's classic *Miss Rumphius* by Barbara Cooney.

❀ *Snapdragons*. My favorite is 'Sonnet,' 14 inches tall and pink. The secret to an abundant bloom is letting the first show of flowers bloom a short while, then pinching off the flowers. This causes the plants to get bushy and produce more flowers. It is worth the initial sacrifice.

❀ *Salvia*, 'Indigo Spires' or 'Purple Majesty.'

❀ *Heliotrope* is dark purple and fragrant and needs part shade.

❀ *Delphinium*

❀ *Lavender*

❀ *Penstemon*

❀ *Topiaries*

❀ *Hollyhocks*

❀ *Blue hibiscus*

❀ *Japanese maples*

❀ *Alstroemeria*

SHADE FAVORITES

❀ *Impatiens*, which bloom abundantly in the shade. Once the weather gets cold, pinch them back and they will re-bloom in the spring.

❀ *Primrose*, different forms and colors—all lovely.

❀ *Cyclamen*

❀ *Hydrangea*

❀ *'Forget-Me-Nots'*

❀ *Azaleas*

❀ *Camellias*

❀ *Japanese anemone*

❀ *Ferns*

❀ *Coleus*

PEST, DISEASE, AND WEED CONTROL

The best treatment for disease and pest control is prevention. Since this book is not totally devoted to roses, this is an abbreviated list of pest, disease, and weed control. You might want to further consult a basic rose book for more in-depth discussion of these subjects, as well as rose pruning and planting.

By working in your garden and being observant, you will notice small problems before they get out of control. I like to make "official" garden rounds at least weekly, with notebook in hand. And, of course, I am in the garden daily. I prioritize the necessary tasks, delegate what I can, and make sure to follow up. Needless to say, keeping your garden debris cleaned up is of utmost importance.

Still, since we're not going to use chemicals, this is what I recommend:

❀ For aphids, squirt them off with a strong spray of water. Repeat if necessary. Then try an application of ladybugs. If still present, use the organic alternative Safer® Brand Insect Killing Soap. This works by denaturing the covering of the insect so that it dies of dehydration.

❀ Do you know what skeletonized rose leaves look like? Well, they have been visited by the rose sawfly, which is a tiny, pudgy wasp, brown/black/purple in color. They lay eggs that become bristly rose slugs, which are tiny green worms that live on the undersides of rose leaves and eat them until all that is left is the skeleton. Their damage can be devastating. To control these evil worms, spray the undersides of the leaves with neem oil, which will smother them, or insecticidal soap. The other cause of skeletonized rose leaves is the Chinese rose beetle. These damaging critters come out from under the soil or debris at the base of plants as the sun sets. Apparently, the way to discourage them is with lights—solar powered pathway lights and strings of overhead Christmas lights (solar powered or on a timer).

❀ Handpick snails. Our ducks' favorite treat was an offering of snails. Chickens also enjoy them, but how many snails can one chicken eat? Anyway, it's kind of the ultimate form of recycling.

❀ I have found beneficial insects to be a very important part of organic garden care. I use ladybugs, lacewings, and trichogramma wasps in March or April and again in June or July. The eggs of lacewings come on little cards that are to be distributed around the garden. The eggs that hatch eat soft-bodied insects such as whitefly, mealybugs, aphids, and young scale. Trichogramma wasps are tiny, stingless wasps that are known as parasitoids. They lay their eggs into the eggs of moths and butterflies, which are leaf eaters in their caterpillar stage (i.e., cutworms).

- Worms also respond nicely to *Bacillus thuringiensis* found under the trade name DiPel® or Safer® Brand Caterpillar Killer.
- For rust and black spot, which are both caused by fungi, handpick the leaves and dispose of them. I never use anything stronger than Safer® Brand Insecticidal Soap or Fungicide. I understand that neem oil is a great antifungal, which prevents and minimizes the most common fungal rose diseases of black spot, rust, and mildew.

- Weeds are Mother Nature's way of covering the ground. When the ground is bare, it loses nutrients, blows away, develops cracks, and weakens structurally. To prevent bare ground, plant closely, plant ground covers, and add a 4-to-6-inch layer of mulch (keeping the crown open around your roses). Weeds are controlled by hoeing or hand pulling. Yes, really.
- To control fleas, I spray nematodes on the lawn every six weeks. This is more frequent than usually recommended, but it controls the problem.

HOMEMADE RECIPES FOR FUNGAL ROSE PROBLEMS

1. Per 1 gallon of water, mix in 1 teaspoon baking soda, 1 tablespoon horticultural or neem oil, and 1 squirt of liquid dish soap. Add to a spray bottle and spray on leaves. If using for rust, be sure to spray the underside of the leaves.

2. Per 1 gallon of water, mix in 1 teaspoon vegetable oil, plus 1 generous squirt of liquid dish soap. Add to a spray bottle and spray on leaves.

TOP LEFT: Aphids. BOTTOM, LEFT: Chinese rose beetles. BOTTOM: Rose leaf skeletonized by Chinese rose beetle. Photo credit: Baldo Villegas.

COMPANION PLANTS

Companion planting is a practice that takes advantage of a mutually beneficial relationship between plants primarily used to combat garden pests and attract beneficial insects. The flowers add to the beauty of the garden and complement veggies and roses. I invite you to explore this practice—there are many possibilities.

In Your Vegetable Garden
Marigolds, calendulas, nasturtiums, petunias, and zinnias are most beneficial planted throughout the garden.

In Your Rose Garden
Companions for roses can be used to add to the beauty of your garden design, provide you with flowers when roses are not in bloom, and create a cottage garden look. For example, foxglove, delphinium, Canterbury bells, larkspur, catmint, lavender, verbena, iris, perennial nemesia, alstroemeria, lobelia, and *Brachycome* are all good choices.

To Repel Insects or Attract Beneficial Insects
Petunias, parsley, sweet alyssum, garlic, marigolds and calendulas, coreopsis, yarrow, and borage.

Clematis with rose, 'Cl. Pinkie' (Climber, 1952)

WORKS *Cited, Permissions* GRANTED

Every effort has been made to obtain permission to reprint quotes used.
If any required acknowledgments have been omitted, or rights overlooked, it is unintentional.

Biles, Roy E. *The Complete Book of Garden Magic.* Garden City Publishing Co., Inc, 1935.

Burnett, Frances Hodgson. *The Secret Garden.* Frederick A. Stokes Company, 1911.

Creasy, Rosalind. *The Complete Book of Edible Landscaping.* Counterpoint Press, Penguin Random House, 1982.

Dass, Ram. *Paths to God: Living the Bhagavad Gita.* Harmony, 2005.

Dass, Ram, with Rameshwar Das. *Polishing the Mirror: How to Live from Your Spiritual Heart.* Sounds True, 2013.

Dass, Ram, and Mirabai Bush. *Walking Each Other Home: Conversations on Loving and Dying.* Sounds True, 2018.

Halifax, Roshi Joan. *The Fruitful Darkness: A Journey Through Buddhist Practice and Tribal Wisdom.* Grove Press, 2004.

James, William. *The Varieties of Religious Experiences: A Study in Human Nature.* Longmans, Green & Co, 1902.

Jekyll, Gertrude. *Wood and Garden: Notes and Thoughts, Practical and Critical, of a Working Amateur.* Cambridge University Press, 2011.

Kornfield, Jack. *Buddha's Little Instruction Book.* Bantam Books, 1994.

Longfellow, Henry Wadsworth. *Final Memorials of Henry Wadsworth Longfellow.* Ticknor and Company, 1887.

Murray, Elizabeth. *Cultivating Sacred Space: Gardening for the Soul.* Pomegranate Press, 1997.

Paramahansa Yogananda. *Man's Eternal Quest.* Self-Realization Fellowship, 1982.

Powell, Richard. *Wabi Sabi for Writers.* Adams Media, 2006.

Ramdas, Swami. *In the Vision of God, Vol. II: The Conclusion to the Saga of an Extraordinary Pilgrimage.* Blue Dove Press, 1995.

Valmiki. Translated by William Buck. *Ramayana.* University of California Press, 1981.

Additional SUGGESTED *Reading*

Damrosch, Barbara. *Theme Gardens: Revised Edition*. Workman Publishing Company, 2000.

Das, Krishna. *Flow of Grace: Chanting the Hanuman Chalisa*. Mandala Publishing, 2019.

Dass, Ram with Levine, Stephen. *Grist For The Mill*. Unity Press, 1977.

Easwaran, Eknath. *A More Ardent Fire, From Everyday Love to Love of God*. Nilgiri Press, Blue Mountain Center of Meditation, 1979.

Fukuoka, Masanobu. Translated by Chris Pearce, Tsune Kurosawa, and Larry Korn. *The One-Straw Revolution: An Introduction to Natural Farming*. Rodale Press, 1978.

Gertley, Jan, and Michael Gertley. *The Art of the Kitchen Garden*. Taunton Press, 1999.

Hoyt, Roland Stewart. *Ornamental Plants for Subtropical Regions: A Handbook for Reference*. Livingston Press, 1978.

Johnson, Will. *Rumi's Four Essential Practices, Ecstatic Body, Awakened Soul*. Inner Traditions, 2010.

Ladinsky, Daniel. *Love Poems from God: Twelve Sacred Voices from the East and West*. Penguin Publishing Group, 2002.

Messervy, Julie. *The Inward Garden: Creating a Place of Beauty and Meaning*. Bunker Hill Publishing, 1995.

Mitchell, Stephen, ed. *The Enlightened Heart: An Anthology of Sacred Poetry*. HarperCollins, 1989.

Mitchell, Stephen, ed. *The Enlightened Mind: An Anthology of Sacred Prose*. HarperCollins, 1991.

O'Donohue, John. *Anam Cara, Spiritual Wisdom From The Celtic World*. Bantam Books, 1997.

Oliver, Mary. *New and Selected Poems*. Beacon Press, 1992.

Rumi, Jelaluddin. Translated by Andrew Harvey. *Call to Love, In the Rose Garden*. Sterling Publishing, 2007.

Ryan, Regina Sara (Introduction by). *In Praise of Rumi*. Hohm Press, 1989.

Vyasa. Translated by William Buck. *Mahabharata*. University of California Press, 1973.

This was the fourth (and last) of my veggie gardens. The raised garden bed on the right was built by my friend Dave Nichols—how wonderful to be able to garden comfortably! It was also a great example of organic companion planting.

ACKNOWLEDGMENTS WITH *Deepest Gratitude*

"Let us be grateful to people who make us happy; they are the charming gardeners who make our souls blossom."

—MARCEL PROUST

It has taken 36 years to birth this book. I am so filled with gratitude for so many people. Please forgive me, as I could not express the full depth of my appreciation in this limited space. My soul—and this book, which is a blossom of that soul—would not have reached this harvest without the support and inspiration of the following people:

Inspiration and Support

Peter Gaal

Becky Gaal

Ram Dass

Ganga Ma, Marlene Roeder

Joyanna Ananda

Dassima, Kathleen Murphy

Shaun Patel, M.D.

Tricia West

My Satsang Family of Friends

Steven Lee Jacobs

The board of the Love, Serve, Remember Foundation, especially Rameshwar Das and Mirabai Bush

My Karma "children": Jennifer Sampson, Ronny Gaal, Linda Gaal, and their children

Dino Cordova

In Our Home

Nina Lupe Schuhl, Kristy Clum, Areli Villalobos, Claudia Peterson, and Lidia Bracamontes

Our Beloved Doggies, who brought us joy and unconditional love: Ginkel, Nikki, Rami, Rosie, Daisy, Teddy, Miki and Lama, and now Harvey, the Love Dog.

Creative, Technical, Design, Publishing

Project Manager, Creative Director, Photographer: Rebecca Gaal

Computer Guru: Joel Berkovitz

Editors: Ganga Ma, Marlene Roeder; Loring Robbins; Rebekah Piatte

Graphic Designer: Laura Baxter

Collective Book Studio: Angela Engel and her team

My friends who wrote endorsements for this book

Those who have granted permissions to use their meaningful quotes

In the Garden:
Juan Ornelas Flores "Parocco,"
Camilo Orozco, Francisco Vargas,
and Juan Vargas

Garden Guru: Joe Seals

Nursery Buddies:

Dave Nichols, Green Thumb Nursery

Richard and James Baron,
Baron Brothers Nursery

Raymond Sodomka,
Turk Hessellund Nursery, Montecito, Ca.

For the Love of Roses
Melody O'Leary Namikas

Clair Martin and Syl Arena,
friends who are knowledgeable,
passionate rosarians and speakers.

Scott Klittich, Otto & Sons Nursery

Penny Stanley, Kathy Simpson,
Bobbie Jaedtke, Kristy Clum,
Claudia Peterson, Steven Lee

Members of the Ventura and
Santa Barbara Rose Societies

My 10 favorite rosarians who
contributed to this book, and by their presence,
to my garden

Oscar Esmaili, Royal Bakery,
and Liz Pompilio, Let's Get Cookin'

All the people who attended
"For the Love of Roses" or have enjoyed
repeated visits to my garden,
adding their love and contributing
to the soul of the garden.

If I have omitted anyone, my apologies.
I hold you all in my heart.

ABOUT THE *Author*

Janaki Sandy Gaal is an organic gardener and bhakti yogi. She knew from a young age that she wanted to relieve people's suffering. She followed her heart along this path and became an ICU nurse, also caring for her family, home, and garden with the same passion, compassion, and attention to detail. As a garden designer, consulting rosarian, and host to thousands who have visited her garden, she discovered that helping others connect with the beauty of nature inspires joy and relieves suffering.

Janaki is the spiritual name given to her by her friend and spiritual teacher, Ram Dass, with whom she collaborated on the book *Polishing the Mirror, How to Live from Your Spiritual Heart*, along with Rameshwar Das. Janaki currently lives on Maui surrounded by *ohana* (her spiritual family).

"Everything that I understand,
I understand only because I love."

—LEO TOLSTOY